# NEGRO LAW

I0102012

## OF

# SOUTH CAROLINA,

COLLECTED AND DIGESTED BY

## JOHN BELTON O'NEALL,

**One of the Judges of the Courts of Law and Errors of the said State,**

UNDER A RESOLUTION OF THE STATE AGRICULTURAL SOCIETY OF SOUTH CAROLINA:

Read before them, at their September Semi-Annual Meeting, 1848, at Spartanburg
Court House—by them directed to be submitted to the Governor, with a
request that he would lay it before the Legislature, at its approach-
ing Session, November, 1848, and by him ordered to be
published for the information of the Members.

ISBN: 978-1-63923-770-8

Printed: March 2023

Published and Distributed By:
Lushena Books
607 Country Club Drive, Unit E
Bensenville, IL 60106
www.lushenabks.com

ISBN: 978-1-63923-770-8

TO HIS EXCELLENCY, DAVID JOHNSON,
*Governor and Commander-in-Chief in and over South Carolina.*

This work, passing through your hands to the Legislature of the State, may, I trust, be appropriately dedicated to you, as a slight testimonial of the friendship which, for more than thirty years, at the Bar, on the Bench, in your present high and dignified office, and in all the relations of life, has existed, and I hope ever will exist between us.

JOHN BELTON O'NEALL.

*Springfield, Oct.* 3, 1848.

*To the State Agricultural Society of South Carolina :*

The undersigned, charged with the preparation of a digest of the Law in relation to Negroes, (slave or free,) and directed to make such suggestions of amendment as to him may seem expedient, begs leave to submit the following as the result of an examination of the subject committed to him, so far as his time and opportunity allowed.

JOHN BELTON O'NEALL.

*Springfield, August* 14, 1848.

---

|  | £ | s | d |  | £ |
|---|---|---|---|---|---|
| Proclamation Money, | 133, | 6, | 8, | for | 100 |
|  |  | s | d |  | s | d |
| Currency, |  | 32, | 8, | for | 4, |

# NEGRO LAW OF SOUTH CAROLINA.

## CHAPTER I.

*The Status of the Negro, his Rights and Disabilities.*

SECTION 1. The Act of 1740, sec. 1, declares all negroes and Indians, (free Indians in amity with this Government, negroes, mulattoes and mestizoes, who now are free, excepted) to be slaves:—the offspring to follow the condition of the mother: and that such slaves are chattels personal.

P. L. 103.
7 Stat. 397.

SEC. 2. Under this provision it has been uniformly held, that color is prima facie evidence, that the party bearing the color of a negro, mulatto or mestizo, is a slave: but the same prima facie result does not follow from the Indian color.

The State vs. Harden, (note,) 2 Speer's, 155. Nelson vs Whetmore, 1 Rich'n, 324.

SEC. 3. Indians, and descendants of Indians are regarded as free Indians, in amity with this government, until the contrary be shown. In the second proviso of sec. 1, of the Act of 1740, it is declared that "every negro, Indian, mulatto and mestizo is a slave unless the contrary can be made to appear"—yet, in the same it is immediately thereafter provided—"the Indians in amity with this government, excepted, in which case the burden of proof shall lie on the defendant," that is, on the person claiming the Indian plaintiff to be a slave. This latter clause of the proviso is now regarded as furnishing the rule. The race of slave Indians, or of Indians not in amity to this government, (the State,) is extinct, and hence the previous part of the proviso has no application.

Miller vs. Dawson & Brown, Dudley's Rep. 174. State vs. Belmont, decided in Charleston, Jan, 1848. P. L. 164. 7 Stat. 398.

SEC. 4. The term negro is confined to slave Africans, (the ancient Berbers) and their descendants. It does not embrace the free inhabitants of Africa, such as the Egyptians, Moors, or the negro Asiatics, such as the Lascars.

Gliddon's Egypt. Exparte Ferrett and others, 1 Con. Rep. by Mill. 194–5. The State vs. Scott, 1 Bail. 273. State vs. Hayes, 1 Bail. 276.

SEC. 5. Mulatto is the issue of the white and the negro.

SEC. 6. When the mulatto ceases, and a party bearing some slight taint of the African blood, ranks as white, is a question for the solution of a Jury.

The State vs. Scott, 1 Bail. 274. The State vs. Davis & Hanna, 2 Bail 558. The State vs. Cantey, 2 Hill, 615.

The State vs. Cautey, 2 Hill, 615, 616.  Johnson vs. Boon, 1 Speer's, 270-1. White & Bass vs. the Tax Collector of Kershaw, 3 Rich'n, 136-7-8-9, 140-1. The State vs Davis & Hanna, 2 Bail. 560.  Turner vs. the Tax Collector of Marion, decided in Charleston, Feb. 1841.

SEC. 7. Whenever the African taint is so far removed, that upon inspection a party may be fairly pronounced to be white, and such has been his or her previous reception into society, and enjoyment of the privileges usually enjoyed by white people, the Jury may rate and regard the party as white.

SEC. 8. No specific rule, as to the quantity of negro blood which will compel a Jury to find one to be a mulatto, has ever been adopted. Between ¼ and ⅛ seems fairly to be debateable ground. When the blood is reduced to, or below ⅛, the Jury ought always to find the party *white*. When the blood is ¼ or more African, the Jury must find the party a mulatto.

The State vs. Hayes, 1 Bail. 276.  The State vs. Scott, 1 Bail. 273.  The State vs. Cantey, 2 Hill, 614.

2d Sec. 9th Art. Con. of S. C. Stat. 191.

SEC. 9 The question of color, and of course of caste, arises in various ways, and may in some cases be decided without the intervention of a Jury.  As when a party is convicted and brought up for sentence, or a witness on the stand objected to as a free negro, mulatto, or mestizo, in these cases, if the color be so obvious that there can be no mistake about it, the Judge may refuse to sentence, or may exclude the witness; still if the party against whose color the decision may be made, should claim to have the question tried by a Jury, it must, I apprehend, be so tried.

State vs. B. Scott, 1 Bail, 296. Johnson vs. Boon, 1 Speer's, 270-1. The State vs. Cantey, 2 Hill 614. Cromer vs. Miller, N. P. Decis. Charleston, May, '47.

SEC. 10. There are three classes of cases, in which the question of color, and of course, of caste, most commonly occurs.  1st. Prohibition against inferior Courts, or the Tax Collector.  2d. Objections to witnesses offered to testify in the Superior Courts.  3d. Actions of slander for words charging the plaintiff with being a mulatto.

The State vs. Scott, 1 Bail. 296.

SEC. 11. In the first class, free negroes, mulattoes and mestizoes are liable to be tried for all offences, by a magistrate, and five free holders, (except in Charleston, where two magistrates must sit,) and of course, any person claiming to be white, (over whom, if that be true, they have no jurisdiction,) charged before them criminally, may object to their jurisdiction, and if they persist in trying him or her, may apply for, and on making good the allegation, is entitled to have the writ of prohibition.  It seems if the party submits to have the question of jurisdiction tried by the Inferior Court, he will be concluded.

SEC. 12. The writ of prohibition is generally granted, nisi, on a suggestion sworn to by the relator, by any Judge at Chambers, on notice being given to the Court claiming jurisdiction; but if the fact be uncontroverted, or so plain as not to admit of doubt, that the relator is white, the Judge may at once grant an absolute prohibition.  Generally, however, an issue is ordered to be made up on granting the prohibition, nisi, in which the relator is plaintiff, and on the Jury finding the relator to be a free white person, the prohibition is made absolute.

SEC. 13. In this class, too, the Tax Collectors frequently issue tax executions for capitation taxes, against persons whom they suppose to be free negroes, mulattoes, or mestizoes, ("free persons of color," as they are sometimes loosely called.) If the person or persons against whom they be issued, be not liable to the tax, they may, on a suggestion, move for, and have the writ of prohibition. Burger, Tax Collector. als. Carter, 1 M'Mull. 418.
Johnson vs. Iloon, 1 Speers, 270-1. White & Bass vs. the Tax Collector of Kershaw, 3 Rich'n, 136.

SEC. 14. In such cases, where, from the affidavits accompanying he suggeston, it appears that the relator or relators has or have been received in society as white, and has or have enjoyed the privileges of a white person, or of white people, I have uniformly made the order for prohibition to become absolute, if the Tax Collector did not within a given time, file his suggestions contesting the status of the relator or relators. This course has been adopted, because the Tax Collector has no jurisdiction over the person of the relator, and has no judicial authority whatever to decide the question of caste. His execution is predicated of an assumed fact. He is, therefore, bound to make that good, before he can collect the tax. This course has been found extremely convenient, as it has cut off an immense amount of litigation. For, generally, the Tax Collectors exercise a sound and honest discretion, in pursuing only those cases where there seems to be no room to doubt the degraded caste of the relator or relators.

· SEC. 15: Where, however, there is to be a question as to the color of the relator or relators, the Court may in its discretion cast the burden of proof on the Tax Collector, or the relator. Generally, I think, it should be cast on the Tax Collector, as his execution is the first allegation of the color of the relator. As the issue may result, the writ of prohibition is made absolute or dissolved.

SEC. 16. In all the cases of the first class, the decision is conclusive; in all subsequent cases, civil or criminal. For the prohibition is in the nature of a criminal proceeding, operating *in rem*, and binds not only the parties, but also all the people of the Commonwealth. So it seems, that any decision made in favor of the caste of the relator, as white, may be given in evidence in his favor. See Reporter's note A, to M'Collum vs. Fitzsimons, 1 Rich'n, 254.
M'Collum vs. Fitzsimons, 1 Rich'n, 252.

SEC. 17. In the 2d class, the objection to the competency of the witness, makes the issue collateral, and it is tried instanter, without any formal issue being made up, and the finding is upon the record on trial. The verdict, in such a case, concludes nothing beyond the question of competency in that case. It, however, might be given in evidence for or against the witness, not as conclusive, but as a circumstance having weight in settling the question of status, in all other cases.

SEC. 18. In the 3d class, where justification is pleaded and found, it would seem to forever conclude the Plaintiff from re-agitating the Cromer vs. Miller, N. P. Decis. Charleston, May, 1847.

question. But, where the defence is as usual, that the Defendant had good reason to suspect and believe that the Plaintiff was, as he alleged, a mulatto, in such case. a finding of nominal damages sustains the defence, yet it concludes not the Plaintiff from afterwards averring and proving that he was white.

SEC. 19. Free Indians and their descendants, unmixed by African blood, are entitled to all the privileges of white men, except that of suffrage and office. The former, and of consequence the latter, has been denied to a pure Indian, living among the whites. The foregoing principle resulting from the case cited in the margin, is, I am persuaded, wrong. The term white, ("free white man,") used in our Constitution, is comparative merely: it was intended to be used in opposition to the colors resulting from the slave blood. The case should be reviewed, and I trust the decision will be reversed; for the case in which it was made, will always condemn it. The relator, the Rev. John Mush, was an Indian of the Pawmunki tribe of Indians, in Virginia; he was a soldier of the Revolution, he had as such, taken the oath of allegiance. He was sent out as a Missionary to the Catawbas. He, however, did not reside among them; he lived among the white inhabitants of York District, where he had resided for many years. He was a man of unexceptionable character. Yet, strange to say, he was held not to be entitled to vote. If that decision be right, how long is the objection to prevail? When is the descendant of an Indian to be regarded as white? Is it. that he is not to be so regarded, until a jury shall find him to be white, on account of the great preponderance of the white blood? But the Indian blood, like that of the white, is the blood of freedom; there is nothing degrading in it, and hence, therefore, the Indian and his descendants may well claim to be white within the legal meaning of our Constitution.

SEC. 20. A mestizo is the issue of a negro and an Indian, and is subject to all the disabilities of a free negro and mulatto.

SEC. 21. The burden of proof of freedom rests upon the negro, mulatto, or mestizo, claiming to be free.

SEC. 22. Under the Act of 1740. 1st sec. 1st proviso, and the Act of 1799, it is provided, if any negro, mulatto, or mestizo shall claim his or her freedom, he may on application to the Clerk of the Court of Common Pleas of the District, have a guardian appointed, who is anthorized to bring an action of trespass, in the nature of ravishment of ward, against any person claiming property in the said negro, mulatto or mestizo, or having possession of the same; in which action, the general issue may be pleaded, and the special circumstances given in evidence; and upon a general or special verdict found, judgment shall be given according to the very right of the case, without any

The State ex relatione, John Marsh,(the name should be John Mush,) vs. the Managers of election for York Dist. 1st Bail 215

Miller vs. Dawson and Brown, Dudley's Report, 174, 176. 2d Proviso of 1st Sec. of the Act of 1740, P. L. 164. 7 Stat. 398.

2d Faust, 324.

Wesner     ads. Guardian of Tom Brister, 1st M'. Mull., 135·

regard to defects in the proceeding, in form or substance. In such case, if the verdict be that the ward of the Plaintiff is free, a special entry shall be made declaring him to be free—and the jury is authorized to assess damages which the Plaintiff's ward may have sustained, and the Court is directed to give judgment, and award execution for the damages and cost; but if judgment is given for the Defendant, then the Court is authorized to inflict corporal punishment on the ward of the Plaintiff, not extending to life or limb. Under the 2d sec. of the Act of 1740, it is provided that the Defendant in such action, shall enter into a recognizance with one or more sufficient sureties to the Plaintiff, in such sum as the Court of Common Pleas may direct, conditioned to produce the ward of the Plaintiff, at all times when required by the Court, and that while the action or suit is pending, he shall not be eloigned, abused or misused. *P. L. 164.*

SEC. 23. Under the 1st proviso, the action of trepass in the nature of ravishment of ward, is an action sounding altogether in damages. The finding for the Plaintiff, is altogther of damages, which may be made up of the value of the services of the Plaintiff's ward, and recompense for any abuse, or injury, which he may sustain. For such damages and the costs, the judgment is entered up, and execution issues.

SEC. 24. Under the Act, the Court is authorized, on such finding for the Plaintiff, to make a special entry, that the ward of the Plaintiff is free. This entry ought to recite the action, the finding of the Jury, and then should follow the order of the Court, that the Plaintiff's ward is free, and that he be discharged from the service of the Defendant. This should be spread on the minutes of the Court. This entry is, it seems, evidence of the freedom of the Plaintiff's ward in all other cases, and against all other persons. It is only conclusive. however, against the Defendant; against all other persons, it is *prima facie* merely. Under the 2d sec., the proceeding is by petition, setting out the action brought to recover the freedom of the negro, the possession by the Defendant, with a prayer, that the Defendant enter into the recognizance required by law. If this order be disobeyed, the Defendant may be attached for a contempt, until it be obeyed; or it may be in analogy to the decision under the Trover Act, that the Sheriff might arrest the Defendant under the order, and keep him in custody until he entered into the recogniz-ance. I never knew the order made but once, and that was in the case of Spear and Galbreath, Guardians of Charles, vs. Rice, Harp. 20. In that case, the order was complied with by the Defendant on notice of it. *Rice ads. Spear and Galbreath, Harp. Report, 20.* *The State vs. Hill, 2d Speers, 160.* *Poole vs. Vernon, 2d Hill, 669.*

SEC. 25. The evidence of freedom is as various as the cases.

SEC. 26. Proof that a negro has been suffered to live in a community for years as a freeman, is *prima facie* proof of freedom. *State vs. Harden, 2d Speers, 156, (note.)*

2

Miller,Adm'r. of
Bennett, vs.
Reigne, et al. 2d.
Hill, 292. The
State vs. Hill, 2d
Speers, 161.

SEC. 27. If before the Act of 1820, a negro was at large, without an owner, and acting as a freeman for twenty years, the Court would presume *omnia esse rita acta*, and every muniment necessary to give effect to freedom to have been properly executed.

SEC. 28. This rule applies also, when freedom has been begun to be enjoyed before the Act of 1820, and the 20 years are completed after.

Cooper's Justini-
an Notes. 416.
Salley vs. Beatty,
1. Bay, 260.
Bowers vs. New.
man, 2. M'Mull.
491..2

SEC. 29. Before the Act of 1800, (hereafter to be adverted to,) any thing which shewed that the owner had deliberately parted with his property, and dissolved the *vinculum suvitii*, was enough to establish freedom.

Monk vs. Jen-
kins, 2 Hill, C. R.
13, Rice ads.
Spear and Gal-
breath, Harper's
Law Report 20.

SEC. 30. The validity of freedom depends upon the law of the place where it begins. Hence, when slaves have been manumitted in other States, and are found in this State, their freedom *here*, will depend on the validity of the manumission at the place whence they came.

7 Stat. 442, 443.

SEC. 31. By the 7th, 8th and 9th sections of the Act of 1800, it was provided, that emancipation could only take effect by deed ; that the owner intending to emancipate a slave, should, with the slave, appear before a Justice of the Quorum, and five Freeholders of the vicinage, and upon oath, answer all such questions as they might ask touching the character and capability of the slave to gain a livelihood in an honest way. And if, upon such examination, it appeared to them the slave was not of bad character, and was capable of gaining a livelihood in an honest way, they were directed to indorse a certificate upon the deed to that effect ; and upon the said deed and certificate being recorded in the Clerk's office, within 6 months from the execution, the emancipation was declared to be legal and valid, otherwise, that it was void. The person emancipating was directed by the 8th section, to deliver to the slave a copy of the deed of emancipation, attested by the Clerk, within 10 days after such deed shall have been executed.

SEC. 32. The person emancipating, neglecting or refusing to deliver such copy, was, by the 9th section, declared to be liable to a fine of $50, with costs, to be recovered by any one who shall sue for the same.

SEC. 33. It was also provided by the 9th section, that a slave emancipated contrary to this Act, may be seized, and made property by any one.

1st Bail. 632, 633.

SEC. 34. It was held, for a long time, that when a will directed slaves to be free, or to be set free, that they were liable to seizure, as illegally emancipated. But the cases of Lenoir vs. Sylvester, and Young vs. the same, put that matter right. In them, it was held, that a bequest of freedom was not void, under the Act of 1800—that it could have no effect until the Executor assented—that when he did assent. It was his duty to so assent as to give legal effect to the bequest. As legal owner, he could execute the deed, appear before the Magistrate and Freeholders, answer the questions, and do every act required by the law, and thus make the emancipation legal.

SEC. 35. A slave illegally emancipated, was free, as against the rights of the owner, under the Act of 1800; he could only restore himself to his rights by capture. The Act of 1820, declares that no slave shall be emancipated but by Act of the Legislature. Still it has been held, in Linam vs. Johnson, and many subsequent cases, that if a slave be in any other way emancipated, he may, under the provision of the Act of 1800, be seized as derelict. Linam vs. John-son, 2nd Bail. Monk vs. Jenk-ins, 2 Hill, C. R. 13. 7 Stat. 459.

SEC. 36. The delivery of the deed of emancipation to the Clerk to be recorded, is all the delivery necessary to give it legal effect; and the delivery to the Clerk is equivalent to recording. Monk vs. Jenk-ins, 2 Hill, C. R. 14.-15.

SEC. 37. The Act of 1820, declaring that no slave should hereafter be emancipated, but by Act of the Legislature. introduced a new. and. as I think. an unfortunate provision in our law. All laws unnecessarily restraining the rights of owners are unwise. So far as may be necessary to preserve the peace and good order of the community, they may be properly restrained. The Act of 1800 was of that kind. The Act of 1820. instead of regulating, cut off the power of emancipation. Like all of its class, it has done harm instead of good. It has caused evasions without number. These have been successful, by vesting the ownership in persons legally capable of holding it, and thus substantially conferring freedom. when it was legally denied. Cline vs. Caldwell, 1 Hill, 423. State vs. Single-tary and others, Dudley's Rep. 220. Carmille vs. Admr. of Car-mille et al. 2d McMull, 424. The State vs. Singletary and Rhame, Dud. 220.

SEC. 38. So too. bequests or gifts, for the use of such slaves, were supported under the rule, that whatever is given to the slave belongs to the master. Carmille vs Admr. of Car-mille, 2 McMull, 424.

SEC. 39. Since the Act of 1820. if a negro be at large, and enjoy freedom for twenty years. he or she is still a slave; as an Act of Emancipation passed by the Legislature, will not be presumed. Vingard vs. Pas-salaigue, 2 Strob.

SEC. 40. The Act of 1820. was plainly intended to restrain emancipation within the State; it was. therefore, held by the Court of Appeals. that where a testator directed slaves to be sent out of the State, and there set free. such bequest was good. Frazier vs. Fra-zier, 2 Hill C. R. 305.

SEC. 41. In '41. the Legislature, by a sweeping Act, declared, 1st. That any bequest, deed of trust, or conveyance. intended to take effect after the death of the owner. whereby the removal of any slave or slaves without the State, is secured or intended. with a view to the emancipation of such slave or slaves, shall he void—and the slave or slaves' assets. in the hands of any Executor or Administrator. 2d. That any gift of any slave or slaves, by deed, or otherwise, accompanied by a trust. secret or implied, that the donee shall remove such slaves from the State to be emancipated, shall be void; and directed 11 Stat. 154.

the donee to deliver up the slave or slaves, or account to the distributees, or next of kin, for their value. 3d. That any bequest, gift, or conveyance of any slave or slaves, with a trust or confidence. either secret or expressed, that such slave or slaves shall be held in nominal servitude only, shall be void, and the donee is directed to deliver the slave or slaves, or to account for their value to the distributees, or next of kin. 4th. That every devise or bequest to a slave or slaves, or to any person upon a trust or confidence, secret or expressed, for the benefit of any slave or slaves, shall be void.

Carmille vs. the<br>Admr. of Car-<br>mille, 2d McMull<br>424. SEC. 42. This Act, reversing the whole body of the law, which had been settled by various decisions from 1830, can have no effect on any deed, will, gift, or conveyance, made prior to its passage, 17th December, 1841.

SEC. 43. This Act, it has been always said, was passed to control a rich gentleman in the disposition of his estate. Like everything of the kind, he defeated it, and the expectations of his next of kin, by devising his estate to one of his kindred, to the exclusion of all the rest.

SEC. 44. My experience as a man, and a Judge, leads me to condemn the Acts of 1820 and 1841. They ought to be repealed, and the Act of 1800 restored. The State has nothing to fear from emancipation, regulated as that law directs it to be. Many a master knows that he has a slave or slaves, for whom he feels it to be his duty to provide. As the law now stands, that cannot be done. In a slave country, the good should be especially rewarded. Who are to judge of this, but the master? Give him the power of emancipation, under well regulated guards, and he can dispense the only reward, which either he, or his slave appreciates. In the present state of the world, it is especially our duty, and that of slave owners, to be just and merciful, and in all things to be *exceptione majori.* With well regulated and mercifully applied slave laws, we have nothing to fear for negro slavery. Fanatics of our own, or foreign countries, will be in the condition of the viper biting the file. They, not us, will be the sufferers. Let me, however, assure my countrymen, and fellow-slaveholders, that unjust laws, or unmerciful management of slaves, fall upon us, and our institutions, with more withering effect than anything else. I would see South Carolina, the kind mother, and mistress of all her people, free and slave. To all, extending justice and mercy. As against our enemies, I would say to her, *be just, and fear not.* Her sons faltered not on a foreign shore; at home, they will die in the last trench, rather than her rights should be invaded or despoiled.

SEC. 45. Free negroes, mulattoes, and mestizoes, are entitled to all the rights of property, and protection in their persons and property, by action or indictment, which the white inhabitants of this State are entitled to.

SEC. 46. They are legally *sui juris*. (The Act of '22 section 8, 7 Sat. 462. requires every male free negro, above the age of 15, to have a guardian, who must be a respectable freeholder of the District, who may be appointed by the Clerk.) Notwithstanding this provision, the free negro is still, as I have said, *sui juris*, when of and above the age of 21. The guardian is a mere protector of the negro, and a guarantor of his good conduct to the public.

Sec. 47. They may contract, and be contracted with. Their marriages with one another, and even with white people, are legal.— Bowers vs. Newman, 2d McMull, 472. They may purchase, hold, and transmit, by descent, real estate.— Real Estate of Mrs. Hardcastle, They can mortgage, aliene, or devise the same. They may sue, and ads. the Escheator of Phœville, be sued, without noticing their respective guardians. reported in the arg't. Bowers

SEC. 48. They are entitled to protect their persons by action, indictment, and the writ of Habeas Corpus, (except that the writ of McMull.479--480. Habeas Corpus is denied to those who enter the State contrary to Harden. note A. the Act of 1835.) They cannot repel force by force; that is, they cannot strike a white man, who may strike any of them. vs. Newman, 2d The State vs. 2 Speers. 152. The State vs. Hill, Idem, 150.-151. The State vs. B.

SEC. 49. It has, however, been held, in a case decided in the Court of Appeals, and not reported, that insolence on the part of a free negro, would not excuse an Assault and Battery. From that decision, I dissented, holding as in the State vs. Harden, 2d Speers (note) 155, "That words of impertinence or insolence addressed by a free negro to a white man, would justify an Assault and Battery." "As a general rule, I should say, that whatever, in the opinion of the Jury, would induce them, as reasonable men, to strike a free negro, should in all cases be regarded as a legal justification, in an indictment." Scott, 1 Bail 294. 1st sec. Act of 1844, 11 Stat.293.

SEC. 50. In addition to the common law, remedies, by action of Assault and Battery, and False Imprisonment, and indictments for the same, the Act of '37 furnishes another guaranty for the protection of free negroes, mulattoes, or mestizoes, by declaring any one convicted of their forcible abduction, or assisting therein, to be liable to a fine not less than $1000, and imprisonment not less than 12 months. 6 Stat. 674.

SEC. 51. Free negroes, mulattoes, and mestizoes, cannot be witnesses or jurors in the Superior Courts. They can be jurors no where. They cannot even be witnesses in Inferior Courts, with the single exception of a Magistrate's and Freeholders' Court, trying slaves or free negroes, mulattoes or mestizoes, for criminal offences and then without oath. This was however, not always the case, to the entire extent which I have stated. It was at one time held, that any *person of color*, if the issue of a free white woman, is entitled to give evidence, and ought to be admitted as a witness, in our Courts. This was predicated of a clear mistake of the civil law maxim of *partus sequitur ventrem*, and of the provision in the 1st section of the Act of 1740, that the offspring should follow the condition of the mother, which only mean, that slavery or freedom should be the condi- White vs. Holmes, McC. 430. Groning vs. Devana. 2d Bail. 192, 13th and 14th sec. of Act of 1740, P. 1, 166. The State vs. Dowell, 2 Brev. 146. The State vs. R. Scott, 1 Bail.273. The State vs. Hays, 1 Bail. 275.

tion of the offspring; but where the words mulatto or mestizo are ever used as designating a class, they are to be interpreted by their common acceptation.

P. L. 166-167.
7 Stat. 401-402.

SEC. 52. It is singular that the 13th and 14th sections of the Act of 1740, directing who may be witnesses against slaves, free negroes, &c., should have been confined to free Indians and slaves, who are to be examined without oath. From which it would seem, that free negroes, mulattoes, &c., might be examined in such cases, as at common law, upon oath. But the practice under the Act has been uniform, as I have before stated it. I think it a very unwise provision, and course of practice, to examine any witnesses in any court, or case, without the sanction of an oath. Negroes, (slaves or free) will feel the sanctions of an oath, with as much force as any of the ignorant classes of white people, in a Christian country. They ought, too, to be made to know, if they testify falsely, they are to be punished for it, by human laws. The course pursued on the trial of negroes, in the adduction and obtaining testimony, leads to none of the certainties of truth. Falsehood is often the result, and innocence is thus often sacrificed on the shrine of prejudice.

Glenn vs. Lopez,
Harp. Rep. 109.

SEC. 53. Free negroes, mulattoes, and mestizoes, may make all necessary affidavits on collateral matters, in cases in the Superior Courts, in which they may be parties, as on motions of postponement, &c. So too, they may in such Court take the oaths under the Insolvent Debtor's or Prison Bounds Act, and under the Acts of Congress to obtain a pension.

Act of '47, p. § 426,
The State v.
Graham. 2d Hill,
457. 2d sec. Act
of '45, 11 Stat. 343.

SEC. 54. Free negroes, mulattoes, and mestizoes, (except such as are proved to the satisfaction of the Tax Collector, to be incapable of making a livelihood,) are liable to a capitation tax, (fixed by each tax Act;) they may make a return personally—or any member of the family may make a return for the rest; or if one be sick, he or she may make such return by agent. They are liable to be double taxed for not making a return of themselves.

Acts of 1805. p. 6.
Act of '33, 2d
sec. p. 4. The
State vs. Graham, 2d Hill,
458.

SEC. 55. This tax seems to have originated in 1805. The Act of 1833 directs the issuing of executions against free negroes, mulattoes and mestizoes, who may fail to pay the tax, and that under them, they may be sold for a term, not exceeding one year; provided, however, that they shall in no instance be sold for a longer term than may be necessary to pay the taxes due; but they cannot be sold under the double tax executions to be issued against them for not making returns of themselves. Such executions go against property merely. The constitutionality of the provision for the sale of free negroes in payment of their taxes, is exceedingly questionable.

2d sec. 9th Art.
Con. S. C.

SEC. 56. The term "free person of color," used in many of our Acts, since 1840, has given rise to many imperfect and improper notions. Its meaning is confirmed by the Act of 1740, and all proper constructions of our *code noir* to *negroes. mulattoes and mestizoes.* In common parlance, it has a much wider signification, *hence the danger of its use*; for all who have to execute the Acts of the Legislature are not *learned lawyers*, or Judges. The Legislature ought to use the words of the Act of 1740. " Free negroes, mulattoes and mestizoes," and then every one would have a certain guide to understand the words used.

SEC. 57. The Act of '35, declares it to be unlawful for any free negro, or *person of color*, to migrate into this State, or to be brought or introduced within its limits, by land or water. <sup>Act of 1835. 1st sec. 7 Stat. 470.</sup>

SEC. 58. Any free negro, or person of color, not being a seaman on board any vessel arriving in this State, violating this law, shall and may be seized by any white person, or by the Sheriff or Constable of the district, and carried before any Magistrate of the district. city or parish—who is authorized to bail or commit the said free negro—and to summon three freeholders, and form a Court for the trial and examination of the said free negro, or person of color, within six days after his arrest; and on conviction. order him to leave the State—and at the time of conviction, to commit him to jail, until he can leave the State, or to release him on bail. not longer than 15 days. And. if after being bailed and ordered to leave the State, the free negro or person of color, shall not leave within 15 days, or having left shall return, shall be arrested, and on conviction before a Court of one Magistrate and three freeholders, he shall be liable to such corporal punishment as the court shall order; if after such punishment, the offender shall still remain in the State "longer than the time allowed," (which is. I suppose, the time previously fixed. 15 days.) or shall return, upon proof and conviction before a court of one Magistrate and three freeholders, the free negro or person of color may be sold, and the proceeds appropriated, one half to the use of the State, the other half to the use of the informer.

SEC. 59. If the free negro or person of color come into this State, on board any vessel, as a cook, steward, mariner, or in any other employment, the Sheriff of the district is to apprehend, and confine in jail, such free negro or person of color, until the vessel be hauled off from the wharf, and ready for sea. The Act provides. that on the apprehension of any free negro or person of color, on board any vessel, the Sheriff shall cause the Captain to enter into a recognizance with good and sufficient security, in the sum of $1000 for each free negro or person of color, who may be on board his said vessel, that he will comply with the requisitions of this Act. which are, that he will. when ready for sea, carry away the said free negro or person of color. and pay the costs of his detension; but if the Captain be unable or refuse so to do, he is to be required by the Sheriff to haul his vessel in the stream, 100 yards distance from the shore, and there remain until ready for sea. If this be not complied with, in 24 hours. <sup>2d sec. 7 Stat. 471.</sup>

the Captain is liable to be indicted, and on conviction, is to be fined not exceeding $1000. and imprisoned not exceeding 6 months.

SEC. 60. Whenever any free negro or person of color, shall be apprehended and committed for coming into this State by sea, it is the duty of the Sheriff to call upon some Magistrate to warn the offender, never again to enter the State, and at the time of giving such warning, the Magistrate is to enter the name of such free negro or person of color, in a book to be kept by the Sheriff, with a description of his person and occupation. which book is evidence of the warning, and is to be deposited in the Clerk's office, as a public record. . If the offender shall not depart the State, in case the Captain shall refuse or neglect to carry him or her away, or having departed, shall ever again enter into the State, he or she is liable to be dealt with. and incur the forfeiture prescribed in the 1st sec.

3d sec. 7 Stat. 471.

SEC. 61 If any free negro or person of color, before the passage of the Act of '35, or since, has left, or shall leave the State, they are forever prohibited from returning. under the penalty of the 1st sec.

5th sec. 7 Stat. 472.

SEC. 62. The 8th sec. of the Act, excepts from its operation free negroes and persons of color, coming into the State from shipwreck, but declares them liable to arrest and imprisonment, as provided in the 2d sec., and to incur all its penalties, if within thirty days they shall not leave the State.

8th sec. 7 Stat. 473.

SEC. 63. The 9th sec. excepts free negroes and persons of color, who shall arrive as cooks, stewards or mariners, or in other employment. in any vessel of the United States; or on board any national vessel of the navies of any of the European or other powers in amity with the United States. unless they shall be found on shore, after being warned by the Sheriff to keep on board their vessels. The Act does not extend to free American Indians, free Moors, or Lascars, or other colored subjects beyond the Cape of Goop Hope, who may arrive in any merchant vessel.

9th sec. 7 Stat. 473.

SEC. 64. Free negroes, and *free persons of color*, (meaning of course mulattoes and mestizoes,) are prohibited, (unless they have a ticket from their guardian,) from carrying any fire arms. or other military or dangerous weapons, under pain of forfeiture, and being whipped at the discretion of a Magistrate and three freeholders. They cannot be employed as pioneers, though they may be subjected to military fatigue duty.

11th sec. 7 Stat. 474.

SEC. 65. The first, second, third and fifth sections of the Act of '35, are to my mind, of so questionable policy, that I should be disposed to repeal them. They carry with them so many elements of discord with our sister States, and foreign nations, that, unless they were of paramount necessity, which I have never believed, we should at once strike them out. I am afraid too, there are many grave constitutional objections to them, in whole or in part.

3d paragraph 8th sec. 1st art. Con. U. S.<br>2d. sec. 9th art. Con. S. C.<br>Chapman vs. Miller, 2d Speers 769.

## CHAPTER II.

*Slaves, their Civil Rights, Liabilities, and Disabilities.*

SEC. 1. In a previous part of this digest, I have had occasion incidentally to state the meaning of the civil law maxim, "*partus sequitur ventrem*," and of the provision of the 1st section of the Act of 1740, "the offspring to follow the condition of the mother." Both mean, that the offspring of a slave mother must also be a slave.

SEC. 2. The maxim, as well as the provision of the Act, has a further meaning in relation to property. It determines to whom the issue belongs. The owner of the mother has the same right in her issue, born while she belongs to him, which he has in her. If for example, the person in possession is tenant for life, then such an one takes an estate for life in the issue. If there be a vested estate in remainder, or one which takes effect on the termination of the life estate, the remainder man is entitled to the issue, on the falling in of the life estate, as he is entitled to the mother. If there be no estate carved out beyond the life estate, then as the mother reverts, so also does the issue. M'Vaughter vs. Elder, 2d Brev. Rep. 314. Ellis vs. Shell, Eq. Rep. (DeS.) 611. Geiger vs. Brown, 4 M'C. 418.

SEC. 3. The estate of a tenant for life in slaves, engaged in making a crop, if he die after the 1st of March, is continued by the Act of '89, until the crop be finished, or until the last day of December, in the year in which the tenant dies. P. L. 499. Lenoir vs. Sylvester, Young vs. the same, 1 Bail. 645.

SEC. 4. The issue of a white woman and a negro, is a mulatto within the meaning of that term, and is subjected to all the disabilities of the degraded caste, into which his color thrusts him. The rule "*partus sequitur ventrem*" makes him a free man. The result of mingling the white and negro blood is to make him a mulatto, and that carries with it, the disqualifications heretofore pointed out. The State vs. R. Scott, 1 Bail. 273. The State vs. Hayes, 1 Bail. 275.

SEC. 5. The 1st section of the Act of 1740, declares slaves to be chattels personal.

SEC. 6. The first consequence legally resulting from this provision would have been without any Act of the Legislature, that the stealing of a slave, should be a larceny (grand or petit) at common law.

SEC. 7. But in 1754, an Act was passed, which, by its first section, made it a felony without the benefit of clergy, to inveigle, steal *and* carry away, or to hire, aid or counsel, any person or persons to inveigle, steal *or* carry away, any slave or slaves, or to aid any slave in running away, or departing from his master's or employer's service. P. L. 235. 7 Stat. 426. The State vs. Miles, 2 N. & M'C. 1. The State vs. Whyte, et. al. 2 N. & M'C. 174. The State vs. Covington, 2d Bail. 569.

SEC. 8. This law, beginning in our Colonial times, and made for us by our rulers, given to us by Great Britain, has remained ever since unchanged, and has been sternly enforced as a most valuable safeguard to property. Yet public opinion was gradually inclining to the belief, that its provisions were too sanguinary, and that they might be *safely* mitigated when the torrents of abuse poured upon the The State vs La Creux. 1 M'Mull. 48.3 State vs. M'Coy, 2 Speers, 711. The State vs. John L. Brown, 2 Speers, 129.

State, and the Judge presiding on the trial from abroad, and the free States of the Union, on account of the conviction of a worthless man. John L. Brown. for aiding a slave to run away and depart from her master's service, *stopped the whole movement of mercy.* It is *now*, however, due to ourselves. that this matter should be taken up, the law changed, and a punishment less than death be assigned for the offence.

Sec. 9. Slaves are in our law, treated as other personal chattels, so far as relates to questions of property, or liability to the payment of debts, except that by the county court Act, (which in this respect is perhaps still of force.) slaves are exempted from levy when other property be shown; and also by the Act of '87, for recovering fines and forfeited recognizances. the sheriff is directed to sell under the executions to be issued, every other part of the personal estate, before he shall sell any negro or negroes.

P. L. 379.

P. L. 420.

Sec. 10. In consequence of this slight character which they bear in legal estimation, as compared with real estate. (which has itself, in our State. become of too easy disposition.) slaves are subjected to continual change—they are sold and given by their masters without writing; they are sold by administrators and executors, and by the sheriff, (and may even be sold by constables.) These public sales by administrators, executors or the sheriff, may be for payment of debts or partition—they (slaves) are often sold under the order of the Ordinary, without any inquiry, whether it be necessary for payment of debts or division. This continual change of the relation of master and slave, with the consequent rending of family ties among them. has induced me to think, that if by law, they were annexed to the freeholds of their owners, and when sold for partition among distributees, tenants in common, joint tenants and coparceners. they should be sold with the freehold. and not otherwise—it might be a wise and wholesome change of the law. Some provision. too, might be made, which would prevent, in a great degree, sales for debts. A debtor's lands and slaves, instead of being sold, might be sequestered until, like *rivum radium*, they would pay all his debts in execution, by the annual profits. If this should be impossible on account of the amount of the indebtedness. then either court, law or equity, might be empowered to order the sale of the plantation and slaves together or separately; the slaves to be sold in families.

Act of 1789, P. L. 433.

Sec. 11. Although slaves, by the Act of 1740. are declared to be chattels personal, yet, they are also in our law, considered as persons with many rights, and liabilities, civil and criminal.

Sec. 12. The right of protection, which would belong to a slave. as a human being. is by the law of slavery; transferred to the master.

Sec. 13. A master may protect the person of his slave from injury, by repelling force with force; or by action, and in some cases by indictment.

Tennent vs. Dendy. Dudley's Rep. 83. Helton vs. Caslon, 2d Bail. 98, 99.

SEC. 14. Any injury done to the person of his slave, he may redress by action of trespass, *ri et armis*, without laying the injury done, with a *per quod servitium amisit*, and this even though he may have hired the slave to another.

Caston vs. Murray. Harp 113. Helton vs. Caston, 2d Bail 95. Tennent vs. Dendy, Dudley's Rep. 83.

SEC. 15. By the Act of 1821, the murder of a slave is declared to be a felony, without the benefit of clergy; and by the same Act, to kill any slave, on sudden heat and passion, subjects the offender, on conviction, to a fine not exceeding $500, and imprisonment not exceeding 6 months.

Acts of 1821, p. 12.

SEC. 16. To constitute the murder of a slave, no other ingredients are necessary than such as enter into the offence of murder at common law. So the killing, on sudden heat and passion, is the same as manslaughter, and a finding by the jury on an indictment for the murder of a slave, of a killing on sudden heat and passion, is good, and subjects the offender to the punishment of the act; or on an indictment for the murder of a slave, if the verdict be guilty of manslaughter, it is good, and the offender is to receive judgment under the Act.

The State vs. Cheatwood, 2d Hill, 459. The State vs. Gaffney, Rice's Rep. 432. The State vs. Fleming, decided at Columbia, Spring, 1848.

SEC. 17. An attempt to kill and murder a slave by shooting at him, was held to be a misdemeanor, and indictable as an assault with an intent to kill and murder. This was a consequence of making it murder to kill a slave.

The State vs. Mann, 2 Hill 453.

SEC. 18. The Act of 1841 makes the *unlawful* whipping or beating of any slave, without sufficient provocation by word or act, a misdemeanor, and subjects the offender, on conviction, to imprisonment not exceeding 6 months, and a fine not exceeding $500.

11 Stat. 155.

SEC. 19. This Act has received no judicial construction by our Court of Appeals. It has been several times presented to me on Circuit, and I have given it construction. The terms "shall *unlawfully* whip or beat any slave not under his charge," "without reasonable provocation," seem to me convertible. For if the beating be excusable from reasonable provocation, it cannot be unlawful. So if the beating be either without provocation, or is so enormous, that the provocation can be no excuse, then it is unlawful. What is sufficient provocation by word or deed, is a question for the jury. The question is, whether as slave owners, and reasonable men, if they had been in the place of the defendant, they would have inflicted the whipping or beating which the defendant did? If they answer this question in the affirmative, then the defendant must be acquitted, otherwise, convicted.

SEC. 20. The Acts of 1821 and 1841, are eminently wise, just, and humane. They protect slaves, who dare not raise their own hands in defence, against brutal violence. They teach men, who are wholly irresponsible in property, to keep their hands off the property of other people. They have wiped away a shameful reproach upon us, that we were indifferent to the lives or persons of our slaves. They have had too, a most happy effect on slaves themselves. They know *now*, that the shield of the law is over them, and thus protected, they yield a more hearty obedience and effective service to their masters.

P. L. 173.

SEC. 21. By the last clause of the 37th section of the Act of 1740, it is provided if any person shall wilfully cut out the tongue, put out the eye, castrate, or cruelly scald, burn, or deprive any slave of any limb, or member, or shall inflict any other cruel punishment, other than by whipping, or beating with a horse-whip, cowskin, switch, or small stick, or by putting irons on, or confining or imprisoning such slave, every such person shall, for every such offence, forfeit the sum of £100 current money, equal to $61 23-100. This provision it has been held extends to any cruel beating of a slave.

The State vs.
Wilson. Chev.
Rep. (So. Ca.
Rep.) p. 163.

SEC. 22. The provision is humane, but the punishment is too slight for such scandalous offences.

SEC. 23. To secure convictions under this part of the 37th section, and also where slaves were killed, it was provided, in the 39th section, that if a slave suffered in life or limb, or was cruelly beaten or abused, where no white person was present, or being present, shall neglect or refuse to give evidence—in every such case the owner or person having the care and management of the slave, and in whose possession or power the slave shall be, shall be adjudged guilty, unless he can make the contrary appear by good and sufficient evidence, or *shall, by his own oath, clear and exculpate himself.* This provision has been considered as applicable to trials under the Act of 1821, and a prisoner charged with the murder of a slave, has been allowed to exculpate himself.

P. L. 173.

The State vs.
Rains, 3d McC.
533.

SEC. 24. This is the greatest temptation ever presented to perjury, and the Legislature ought to speedily remove it.

SEC. 25. The 38th section of the Act of 1740, requires the owners of slaves to provide them with sufficient *clothing, covering and food,* and if they should fail to do so, the owners respectively are declared to be liable to be informed against to the next nearest Justice of the Peace, (Magistrate now,) who is authorized to hear and determine the complaint; and if found to be true, or in the absence of proof, if the owner will not exculpate himself by his own oath, the magistrate may make such order as will give relief, and may set a fine not exceeding £20, current money, equal to $13 66-100, on the owner, to be levied by warrant of distress and sale of the offender's goods.

P. L. 173.
7 Stat. 411.

SEC. 26. This provision, it must be remarked, (leaving out the exculpatory part) is a very wise, and humane one, *except that the penalty is entirely too slight.* I regret to say, *that there is in such a State as ours,* great occasion for the enforcement of such a law, *accompanied by severe penalties.* It might be proper, that this matter should by the direction of an Act, hereafter to be passed, be given in charge to the Grand Jury, at each and every term, and they be solemnly enjoined to enquire of all violations of duty, on the part of masters, owners, or employers of slaves, in furnishing them with sufficient clothing, covering, and food; and the law might also direct that every one by them reported, should be ordered instantly to be indicted.

SEC. 27. It is the settled law of this State, that an owner cannot abandon a slave needing either medical treatment, care, food or raiment. If he does, he will be liable to any one who may furnish the same. In Fairchild vs. Bell, that good man, and great Judge, Wilds. whose early death, South Carolina had good cause to deplore, said, in the noble language of a Christian and patriot, "the law would infer a contract against the evidence of the fact, to compel a cruel and capricious individual to discharge that duty, which he ought to have performed voluntarily. For as the master is bound by the most solemn obligation to protect his slave from suffering, he is bound by the same obligation to defray the expenses or services of another to preserve the life of his slave, or to relieve the slave from pain and danger. *The slave lives for his master's service. His time, his labor, his comforts, are all at his master's disposal.* The duty of humane treatment and of medical assistance, (when clearly necessary) ought not to be withholden.

<small>Fairchild vs.<br>Bell, 2 Brev.<br>Rep. 129.<br><br>City Council vs.<br>Cohen. 2d<br>Speer's, 408.</small>

SEC. 28. By the 22nd section of the Act of 1740, slaves are protected from labor on the Sabbath day. The violation of the law in this respect subjects the offender to a fine of £5 current money, equal to $3 7-100, for every slave so worked.

<small>P. L 168.<br>7 Stat. 404 ✓</small>

SEC. 29. By the 44th section of the same Act. owners or other persons having the care and management of slaves, are prohibited from working or putting the said slaves to work for more than 15 hours from the 25th March to 25th September, and 14 hours from 25th September to 25th March, under a penalty of £20 current money, equal to $13 66-100 for every offence.

<small>P. L. 174.<br>7 Stat. 413.<br><br>ᐟ</small>

SEC. 30. The time limited and allowed for labor in this section is too much. Few masters now demand more than 12 hours labor from 1st March to 1st October, and 10 hours from the 1st October to 1st March. This, after allowing suitable intervals for eating and rest, is about as much as humane prudent masters will demand.

SEC. 31. A slave may, by the consent of his master, acquire and hold *personal* property. All, thus acquired, is regarded in law as that of the master.

<small>Hobson vs. Perry. 1 Hill. 277.<br>Carmille vs. the Adm'r. of Carmille, 2 McMull</small>

SEC. 32. The only exception is under the 34th section of the Act of 1740, which makes goods acquired by traffic and barter for the particular and peculiar benefit of such slave, boats, canoes, or periaugers in the possession of a slave, as his own, and for his own use; horses. mares, neat cattle, sheep or goats, kept, raised or bred for the use of any slave, liable to be seized by any one, and forfeited by the judg-

<small>P. L. 171.<br>The State vs. Mazÿck,3d Rich. 291<br>Norwood vs. Mazÿck, 3d Rich. 296.</small>

ment of any Justice (magistrate) before whom they may be brought.

Richardson vs.
Brough on. Cola.
Spring, 1848.  1
Law Reporter,
new series, 120.
Clarke ads.
Blake. 3d McC.
179.

SEC. 33. Under this section, it has been lately held, that no one can enter on the plantation of the master to make such seizure.

SEC. 34. A seizure can therefore only be made when a slave is [bond; as owner, in possession of the contraband articles, outside of his master's plantation.

SEC. 35. This qualification may render the law harmless. Still it ought to be repealed. The reasons which led to its enactment have all passed away. It is only resorted to, now, to gratify the worst passions of our nature. The right of the master, to provide as comfortably as he pleases for his slave, could not be, and ought not to be abridged in the present state of public opinion. The law may very well compel a master to furnish his slave with proper, necessary, wholesome, and abundant raiment and food ; but certainly no legislator now, would venture to say to a master, you shall not allow your slave to have a canoe to fish with, or to carry vegetables to market or that he should not be allowed to have a horse to attend to his duties as a stock-minder in the swamps, savannas, and pine forests of the lower part of the State, or that a family of slaves should not have a cow to furnish them with milk, or a hog to make for them meat, beyond their usual allowance. All these are matters between the master and the slave. in which neither the public nor any prying, meddling, mischievous neighbor, has any thing to do. Experience and observation fully satisfy me that the first law of slavery is that of kindness from the master to the slave. With that properly inculcated, enforced by law. and judiciously applied, slavery becomes a

2 Moultrie's
Mem. 355.-356.

family relation. next in its attachments to that of parent and child.— It leads to instances of devotion on the part of the slave, which would do honor to the heroism of Rome herself.* With such feelings on our plantations, what have we to fear from fanaticism? Our slaves would be our sentinels to watch over us ; our defenders to protect our firesides from *those prowling harpies, who preach freedom, and steal slaves from their happy homes.*

SEC. 36. A slave cannot contract, and be contracted with. This principle was broadly laid down by the Constitutional Court, in a

Gregg vs. Thomson,2d Con. Rep.
(Mill 331.)

case in which a note was given by the defendant to the plaintiff's slave by name. and the plaintiff brought the action upon it. From this decision, Judge Cheves dissented, upon. I presume, the ground that the master had the right to affirm the contract, and make it his own, and consider it for his own benefit. In it. I think, he was right, on

---

* In 1812, February, Professor Chas. Dewar Simmons on his return to Columbia from Charleston, found the Haughabook Swamp entirely over the road. In attempting to cross on horseback, he was washed off the road and separated from his horse. He first succeeded in reaching a tree. then constructed a raft of rails tied with his comfort. Three times his slave Marcus, swam in to his rescue. His master told him he could not help him, save himself; but he persisted until both perished together.

the principle that the acquisition of the slave is his master's, and that a slave's contract is like an infant's with an adult. It is not binding on the slave; but if the master affirm it, the defendant cannot be discharged.

SEC. 37. A slave cannot even legally contract marriage. The marriage of such an one is morally good, but in point of law, the union of slave and slave, or slave and free negro, is concubinage *merely.*

SEC. 38. The consequence is, that the issue of a marriage between a slave and a free negro, are illegitimate, and cannot inherit from father or mother, who may be free.

The hardship of such a case, where the issue of free negroes married to one another can inherit, might very well lead to a judicious enactment to remedy it.

SEC. 39. A slave cannot testify, except as against another slave, free negro, mulatto, or mestizo, and that without oath. 13 and 14th sec. of Act of 1740. P. L. 166--7.

SEC. 40. The propriety of this is *now* so doubtful, that I think the Legislature would do well to repeal this provision, and provide that slaves in all cases against other slaves, free negroes, mulattoes, and mestizoes, may be examined *on oath.* 7 Stat. 401--2.

SEC. 41. By the Act of 1834, slaves are prohibited to be taught to read or write, under a penalty (if a white person may offend) not exceeding $100 fine and six months imprisonment, if a "*free person of color,*" not exceeding 50 lashes and a fine of $50. Acts of '34, p 13. P. L. 174. 45th sec. of 1740.

SEC. 42. This Act grew out of a feverish state of excitement produced by the *impudent* meddling of persons out of the slave States, with their peculiar institutions. That has, however, subsided, and I trust we are now prepared to act the part of wise, humane and fearless masters, and that this law, and all of kindred character, will be repealed. When we reflect, *as Christians, how can we justify it, that a slave is not to be permitted to read the Bible?* It is in vain to say there is danger in it. The best slaves in the State, are those who can and do read the Scriptures. Again, who is it that teach your slaves to read? It generally is done by the children of the owners. Who would tolerate an indictment against his son or daughter for teaching a favorite slave to read? *Such laws look to me as rather cowardly.* It seems as if we were afraid of our slaves. Such a feeling is unworthy of a Carolina master.

SEC. 43. The 2d section of the Act of 1834, prohibits the employment of a slave, or free person of color, as a clerk or salesman, under a penalty not exceeding $100 fine, and imprisonment not exceeding 6 months. 7 Stat. 468--469.

SEC. 44. The 1st section of the Act of 1800, prohibits the assemblies of slaves, free negroes, mulattoes or mestizoes, with or without white persons, in a confined or secret place of meeting, or with gates 7 Stat. 440--1.

or doors of such place of meeting barred or bolted, so as to prevent the free ingress and egress to and from the same ; and Magistrates, Sheriffs. Militia Officers and Officers of the patrol, are authorized to enter, and if necessary, to break open doors, gates, or windows, (if resisted) and to disperse the slaves, free negroes. mulattoes or mestizoes, found there assembled. And the officers mentioned in the Act are authorized to call such force and assistance from the neighborhood, as they may deem necessary ; and may, if they think necessary, impose corporal punishment on such slaves, free negroes. mulattoes, or mestizoes, and if within Charleston, they may deliver them to the Master of the Work House. who is required to receive them and inflict any such punishment as any two Magistrates of the City may award, not exceeding 20 lashes. If out of the City, the slaves. free negroes, mulattoes and mestizoes found assembled contrary to this Act, may be delivered to the nearest Constable, who is to convey them to the nearest Magistrate, and to inflict under his order, punishment not

exceeding 20 lashes.

SEC. 45. The 2d section of the Act of 1800, which prohibited meetings for the religious or mental instruction of slaves, or free negroes, mulattoes or mestizoes, before the rising of the sun, or after the going down of the same, was very properly altered by the Act of 1803, so as to prohibit the breaking into any place of meeting, wherein the
members of any religious society are assembled, before 9 o'clock at night, provided a majority are white people. After 9 o'clock at night, or before. if the meeting be composed of a majority of negroes, (although white persons may be present.) it may be dispersed by Magistrates, Sheriffs, Militia Officers, and Officers of the patrol, and slaves, free negroes, mulattoes and mestizoes may be punished not

exceeding 20 lashes.

    SEC. 46. In the case of Bell ads. Graham. it was held that these Acts could not justify a patrol in intruding on a religious meeting, *in the day time*, in an open meeting-house, where there were some white people, although there might be a majority of negroes.

    SEC. 47. The 2d section of the Act of 1800. and the amendatory Act of 1803, are treated now, as dead letters. Religious meetings of negroes. with only one or more white persons, are permitted by night as well as by day. They ought to be repealed. They operate as a reproach upon us in the mouths of our enemies, in that we do not afford our slaves that free worship of God, which he demands for all his people. They, if ever resorted to, are not for doing good, but to gratify hatred, malice, cruelty or tyranny. This was not intended, and ought to have no countenance or support, in our Statute law.

    SEC. 48. The 40th section of the Act of 1740, regulates the apparel of slaves, (except livery men or boys) and prohibits them from wearing any thing finer, other or of greater value than negro cloth;

duffils, kerseys, osnaburgs, blue linen, check linen, or *coarse garlix*, p. L. 173. or calicoes, checked cottons or Scotch plaids; and declares all garments of finer or other kind, to be liable to seizure by any constable as forfeited.

SEC. 49. This section has not. within my knowledge, ever been enforced. Indeed, if enforced now, it would make an immense booty to some hungry, unprincipled seeker of spoils. It ought to be repealed.

SEC. 50. The 42d section of the Act of 1740, prohibits a slave or p. L. 174. slaves from renting or hiring any house, room, store or plantation, on his own account. Any person offending against this Act, by renting or hiring to a slave or slaves. is liable to a fine of £20 currency. equal to $13 66-100, to be recovered on complaint made to any magistrate. as is directed in the Act for the trial of small and mean P. L. 213. causes.

SEC. 51. The 43d section of the Act of 1740; which declares it to p. L. 174. be unlawful for more than 7 male slaves in company, without some white person accompanying them, to travel together any of the public roads. and on doing so. makes it lawful for any white person to take them up and punish them by whipping, not exceeding 20 stripes, is, I am afraid, of force. unless it be considered as impliedly repealed by the restriction on the patrol, to whip slaves found out of their 13th sec. of Act owner's plantation without a ticket in writing. of '39, 11 Stat. 60.

SEC. 52. The occasion for such a law has passed away. Public opinion has considered it unnecessary, and like every useless severity, mercy has condemned it. It would be well that it should be repealed.

SEC. 53. The Act of 1819, 5th section, repeals the 23d section of Acts of 1819 p. the Act of 1740. The law now, makes it unlawful for any slave, 31. P. L. 163. except in the company and presence of some white person, to carry or The State vs. make use of any fire arms or other offensive weapon, without a ticket 291. Cattel, 2d Hill, or license. in writing. from his owner or overseer; or unless such slave be employed to hunt and kill game, mischievous birds or beasts of prey, within the limits of his master's plantation. or unless such slave shall be a watchman in and over his owner's fields and plantation. If this law be violated, any white person finding a slave carrying or using a gun or other offensive weapon, without a ticket or license in writing, from his owner or overseer, or not used to hunt game, &c. within the plantation. or as a watchman in the same, may seize and appropriate to his own use, such gun or offensive weapon. But to make the forfeiture complete and legal. the party making the seizure. must, within 48 hours after the seizure, go before the next Magistrate. and make oath of the manner of taking, and then, after 48 hours notice to the owner or overseer having charge of the slave, by summons to shew cause why the articles should not be condemned, (the service of the summons being proved on oath,) the Magistrate

4

may, by certificate under his hand and seal. (if he be satisfied that the arms have been seized according to the Act of 1819) declare the same to be forfeited.

7 Stat. 462.
Sec. 54. The 6th section of the Act of 1822 declares it to be unlawful to hire to male slaves their own time; and if this law be violated, the slaves are declared liable to seizure and forfeiture according to the provisions of the Act in the case of slaves coming into this State.

Sec. 55. Whether this provision relates to the 4th section of the Act of 1816, 7 Stat. 453, or to the 5th section of the Act of 1803, 7 Stat. 450, is indeed somewhat uncertain. The Act of 1816, and all its provisions were repealed by the Act of 1818, 7 Stat. 458. The Act of 1803, seems to be unrepealed, and hence, therefore, I presume the proceeding to forfeit must be under it. By it the proceeding is to be in the name of the State, in the nature of an action of detinue.

P. L. 172.
Sec. 56. The latter part of the 36th section of the Act of 1740, declares that any master, or overseer, who shall permit or suffer his or their negro or other slave or slaves, at any time to beat drums, blow horns, or use any other loud instruments, or whosoever shall suffer and countenance any public meeting or feastings of strange negroes or slaves, on their plantation, shall forfeit £10 current money, equal to $6 88-100 upon conviction; or proof, provided information or suit be commenced within one month.

Sec. 57. This provision is one so utterly unnecessary, that the sooner it is expunged from the Statute book, the better. Indeed it is not only unnecessary, but it is one under which most masters will be liable, whether they will or not. Who can keep his slaves from blowing horns or using other loud instruments?

7 Stat. 450.
Sec. 58. The 2d section of the Act of 1803, prohibits the importation of any negro, mulatto, mestizo, or other person of color, bond or free, from the Bahama, West India Islands, or South America, and also from other parts, of all of those persons who have been resident in any of the French West India Islands.

Sec. 59. The 3d section provides that no male slave above the age of 15 years shall be brought into this State from any of our sister States, unless the person importing such negro shall produce and file in the office of the Clerk of the District, where the person so importing may reside, a certificate under the hands of two magistrates, and the seal of the Court of the District where the slave so imported resided for the last twelve months previous to the date of the certificate, that he is of good character, and has not been concerned in any insurrection, or rebellion.

Sec. 60. Under the 5th section, if slaves be brought into this State in violation of the provisions of the 2nd and 3d sections, they are declared to be forfeited, one half to the State, the other half to the informer; to be recovered in the name of the State, by action in the nature of an action of detinue. in which it is not necessary to prove that the defendant was in possession. at the commencement of the suit, and the informer is a competent witness.

SEC. 61. The 3d section of this Act has been so often violated, that it could hardly be enforced at present, without great injustice. Still the provision is a wise one. No greater curse has ever been inflicted ✓ on South Carolina, than the pouring upon her of the criminal slaves of our sister States. It might be well for the Legislature, in revising (which I hope they will speedily do) our *Code Noir*, to re-enact this provision.

SEC. 62. The Act of '35, makes it unlawful to bring into this State 6th sec. 7 Stat. originally, or to bring back into this State, after being carried out of 472. it, any slave from any port or place in the West Indies, or Mexico, or any part of South America, or from Europe, or from any sister State, situated to the north of the Potomac River, or city of Washington, under the penalty of $1000, for each slave, to be recovered in an action of debt, and forfeiture of the slave.

This provision does not extend to runaway slaves.

SEC. 63. By the Act of '47, any slave carried out of this State, in the capacity of Steward, Cook. Fireman. Engineer, Pilot, or Mariner, Act of '47, 11 on board any steamer, or other vessel trading with any port or place Stat. 43³. in the Island of Cuba, may be brought back into this State, if he may not in his absence have visited some other port or place in the West Indies other than the Island of Cuba, or a port or place in Europe, Mexico, South America or any State north of the river Potomac and City of Washington.

SEC. 64. The 7th section of the Act of '35, providing for the con- The State vs. demnation and forfeiture of a slave by a Court of a Magistrate and Simmons, et al. Freeholders. was declared by the whole Court of Errors, in the State 2 Speers, 761. vs. Simmons. et al., to be unconstitutional. How the forfeiture declared in the 6th section is to be carried out, is somewhat doubtful. I suppose it might be a part of the judgment on the indictment and conviction of the owner for bringing back a slave, which he had carried to the prohibited places. The whole provision had better be repealed. Slaves visiting free States find nothing to enamour them of negro freedom *there:* in general. after all the *labors of love* of our negro-loving brethren of the free States, they, in general, return to their Southern homes, better slaves. Forfeitures, too, may occur under this Act. which none of us would bear. Every servant, (negro, mulatto. or mestizo.) who has been in Mexico during the war, and who has returned, is liable to be forfeited, and his master to pay a fine of $1000. Could the law be enforced in such a case? We have nothing to fear, if the whole Act of '35 be repealed. It ought to be, for no law should stand, which public opinion, in many cases, would not suffer to be enforced. Indeed there are few, very few cases, where the

Act of '35 could meet with public favor. I speak unreservedly, for I am talking to friends, slave-holders—citizens of a State, whom I love, and whom I would have to be, "without fear, and without reproach."

## CHAPTER III.

*Crimes of Free Negroes, Mulattoes, Mestizoes, and Slaves—Their Punishment and Mode of Trial, including the Law as to Runaways and the Patrol.*

SEC. 1. The general rule is, that whatever would be a crime at common law, or by Statute, in a white person, is also a crime of the same degree, in a free negro, mulatto, mestizo, or slave. In some instances the punishment has been altered, in others new offences have been created. There are also cases, in which the slave or free negro, mulatto or mestizo, from his status, would be guilty of a higher crime than a white person would be. under the same circumstances.

The State vs. Crank, 2d Bail. 76. These will be tried to be fully noticed, in this digest. Whenever a slave commits a crime by the command, and coercion of the master, mistress, owner. employer, or overseer, it is regarded as the crime of the master, mistress, owner, employer, or overseer; and the slave is not criminally answerable.

SEC. 2. A free negro, mulatto or mestizo. cannot lawfully strike any white person, even if he be first stricken, and therefore, if he commit homicide of a white person. generally, he cannot be guilty of manslaughter; he is either guilty of murder. or altogether excused. *I suppose* if one without authority to govern or control a free negro, mulatto, or mestizo, were in the act of endangering life or limb of the free negro. mulatto, or mestizo, and he. to defend himself and save life or limb, were to slay his assailant. *it might* be excusable. A free negro, mulatto, mestizo, or slave, slaying one of the same *status*, would be guilty of murder, manslaughter. or be excused, se defendendo, as in the case of white people. at common law.

P. L. 167. 7 Stat. 402. SEC. 3. The 17th section of the Act of 1740. declares a slave who shall be guilty of homicide of any sort. upon any white person, except it be *by misadventure*, or in defence of his master or other person, under whose care and government such slave shall .be, shall, upon conviction, suffer death.

This seems to conflict in some degree, with what is said. 3d chap. 1st section. Still, I think what is affirmed *there*. is law. A homicide committed by the command and coercion of the master. is not one of which the slave is guilty, but the master is alone guilty of it.

SEC. 4. By the 24th section of the Act of 1740, it is provided, if *a* [P. L. 169. 7 Stat. 405.] slave shall grievously wound. maim, or bruise any white person, unless it be by the command, and in the defence of the person or property of the owner, or other person having the care or government of such slave, such slave on conviction, shall suffer death.

SEC. 5. The 18th section of the Act of 1751 (which having altered [7 Stat. 425. P. L. 312. 1st sec. State vs. Nicholas. Charleston, Jan. 1818, 2 Strob.] the Act of 1740, is by the Act of 1783, continuing the Act of 1740. continued, instead of the parts altered) gives to the Courts trying any negro or other slave, for any offence under the Acts of 1740. or 1751. where any favorable circumstances appear, the power to mitigate the punishment by law directed to be inflicted.

SEC. 6. The meaning of the words grievously wound, maim. or bruise. has never received any precise adjudication. In the case of the State vs. Nicholas. a portion of the Court indicated their opinion to be, that to grievously wound. maim, or bruise. meant such an injury as might endanger life or limb. This is. I think, the true meaning. The subject. before '48 passed under my review, in the unfortunate case, in York. which led to the passage of the Act of '43. In that case. the lady on whose body the outrage was attempted, was seriously bruised. yet so, as in no way to endanger life. I thought, and so decided, that the slave was not guilty of a capital felony.

SEC. 7. By the Act of 1843. any slave or *free person of color.* (mean- [11 Stat. 258.] ing any free negro, mulatto. or mestizo) who shall commit an assault and battery on a white woman, with intent to commit a rape. shall on conviction. suffer death. without the benefit of clergy.

SEC. 8. The 24th section of the Act of 1740. declares any slave, [P. L. 169. 7 Stat. 405] who shall strike any person, unless it be by the command and in defence of the person and property of the master, or other person having the care and government of such slave, for the 1st and 2nd offence. liable to such punishment as the Court may think fit, not extending to life or limb. and for the 3d offence. to the punishment of death. Under the 4th section, and this of the 3d chapter, it ought to be remarked. that *that portion* of the 24th section of the Act of 1740. which exempts a slave from punishment for acting in obedience to his master and in his defence. requires more to make out his exemption than the Act intended. For it not only requires that the striking, wounding, maiming. and bruising. should be under the command of the master. but also in defence of his person or property. Either the command of the owner or other person having the care or government of the slave. the defence of his person or property should be enough. *The law ought to be so amended.* Any slave seeing a white man about to knock his master down, or in the act of stealing his property, ought not to wait for a command—his blow in defence; under such circumstances, is good and ought to be lawful.

P. L. 167.
7 S.at. 350.
Sec. 9. The 16th section of the Act of 1740, provides that any slave, free negro, mulatto, Indian. or mestizo, who shall *wilfully* and *maliciously*, burn or destroy any stack of rice, corn, or other grain, of the produce, growth, or manufacture of this State, or shall wilfully and maliciously set fire to, burn or destroy any tar kiln, barrels of pitch, tar, *turpentine* or rosin, or any other goods or commodities, the growth, produce or manufacture of this State, or shall feloniously steal, take, or carry away any slave, being the property of another, *with intent to carry such slave out of the State*, or shall wilfully and maliciously poison, or administer any poison to any person, *freeman*, woman, servant, or slave, shall suffer death. Over these and all other offences, for which, under the Act of 1740, death may be the punishment, the Court, under the 18th section of the Act of 1751, mentioned in the 5th section of the 3d Chapter of this Digest, have the power of mitigating the punishment. The term Indian, used in this 16th section of the Act of 1740, means either a freed Indian, (one who was once a slave) or an Indian not in amity with this government. (See 3d section of 1st Chap.) In the case of the State vs.

1 N. and McC.
475.
Whyte and Sadler, it was held that the Act of 1754, making it a felony without clergy, to inveigle, steal, or carry away any slave, applied to slaves, as well as to free people, and hence, therefore, that it repeals that provision of the Act of 1740, which made it capital, on the part of a slave, " to steal, take, or carry away any slave, the property of another, *with intent to carry such slave out of the State.* I think the decision very questionable. For in 1783, the Act of 1740 was continued as law, without noticing this supposed repeal of 1754. If the Act of '54 in this respect, and not the Act of '40, is to govern slaves, then every slave aiding another in running away, is liable to be hanged. This certainly is rather a hard consequence.

P. L. 167. 7 Stat.
300, 424, 425.
Sec. 10. By the 17th section of the Act of 1740, and the 14th section of the Act of 1751, amending the same, any slave, who shall raise or attempt to raise an insurrection, or shall delude and intire any slave to run away and leave this State, and shall have actually prepared provisions, arms, ammunition, horse or horses, or any boat, canoe, or other vessel, whereby the guilty intention is manifested, is liable, on conviction, to be hanged, unless the Court, from favourable circumstances, should mitigate the sentence, or from several being concerned, should be disposed to select some, on whom they would inflict other corporal punishment.

P. L. 29th sec.
170–7 S.at, 467.
See. 11. A slave who shall harbor, conceal or entertain any slave that shall run away, or shall be charged or accused with any crimi-

nal matter, shall suffer such corporal punishment, not extending to life or limb, as the Court may direct.

SEC. 12. A free negro, mulatto, or mestizo, who in 29th section of the Act of 1740, was liable to a penalty for harboring a slave, is by the Act of 1821, (which operates as an implied repeal ) if he or she harbor, conceal or entertain any fugitive or run away slave, liable on conviction to such corporal punishment, not extending to life or limb, as the Court may in their discretion think fit.  *Ac's of t8Qt. p 20. 7 Stat. 460, Righton vs. Wood, Dud. 164.*

SEC. 13. The 30th section of the Act of 1740, prohibits any slave residing in Charleston from buying, selling, dealing, trafficking, bartering, exchanging or using commerce for any goods, wares, provisions, grain, victuals of any sort or kind whatsoever, (except slaves who, with a ticket in writing from their owner or employer, may buy or sell fruit, fish and garden stuff, or may be employed as porters, carters, or fishermen—or may purchase any thing for the use of their masters, owners, or other person, who may have the care and government of such slaves in open market.) All goods, wares, provisions, grain, victuals or commodities, in which such traffic by slaves is carried on, are liable to be seized and forfeited; and may be sued for and recovered before any Magistrate of Charleston, one half to the informer, the other half to the poor of the parish of St. Philip's, and the Magistrate by whom the forfeiture is adjudged, is authorized to inflict corporal punishment on the slave engaged in such traffic, not exceeding twenty stripes. The 31st section prohibits any slave belonging to Charleston, from buying any thing to sell again, or from selling any thing on their own account in Charleston. All goods, wares and merchandize purchased or sold in contravention of this section, are liable to be forfeited by the judgment of any Magistrate of Charleston, one half to the use of the poor, the other half to the informer.  *P. L. 170, 171, 7 Stat, 407-8.*   *31st sec Act of 1740, 7 Stat. 409.*

SEC. 14. If any slave, (without the command of his or her master, mistress, or overseer, evidenced by a ticket in writing,) shall shoot or kill between the 1st of January, and the last day of July in each year, any fawn, (deer,) or any buck, (deer,) between the 1st of Sept. and last day of Oct., and between the 1st day of March and last day of April, such slave, upon conviction before a Magistrate, by the oath of a sufficient witness, or the confession of the said slave, shall, by order of the Magistrate, receive 20 lashes on the bare back, unless security be given for the payment within one month of the fine imposed by the Act, on white or free persons, £2 proclamation money, equal to $6 44-100 for each fawn or buck killed. If the slave shall kill a doe, between the 1st day of March, and the 1st of Sept., without the consent and privity of the owner or overseer, such slave is liable, on conviction before a Magistrate and four  *P. L. 275.*   *P. L. 497, 498, 3d and 7th sec. Act of '89.*

freeholders (sworn according to the 4th section) to receive 39 lashes on the bare back.

Sec. 15. A slave detected in fire hunting, or who shall kill in the night-time, any deer. horse or neat cattle, or stock of any kind, not the property of his master or owner, without the privity or consent of the owner or overseer of the said slave, such slave, on conviction before a Court of one Magistrate and four freeholders, sworn to the best of their judgment, without partiality, favor or affection, to try the cause now depending between the State, Plaintiff, and B. the slave of C. Defendant, and a true verdict give, according to evidence, is liable to receive 39 lashes on the bare back.

Sec. 16. Any slave. who, not in the presence and by the direction of some white person, shall mark or brand any horse, mare, gelding, colt, filly, ass, mule, bull, cow, steer, ox, calf, sheep, goat or hog, is liable to be whipped, not exceeding 50 lashes, by the order of any Magistrate before whom the offence shall be proved by the evidence of any white person or slave.

Sec. 17. The Act of 1834, authorizes the Court, before which a slave or free person of color is convicted of any offence, not capital, to punish the offender by imprisonment, provided this Act shall not abolish the punishments which were then by law imposed. Under this Act, the question will arise, whether the punishment by imprisonment is cumulative; or whether, when resorted to, it is in place of the other punishment to which the offender is liable. I incline to the opinion, that the punishment is not cumulative, but may be substituted for other punishment, at the discretion of the Court.

Sec. 18. A slave guilty of insolence to a white person, may be tried by a Court of a Magistrate and freeholders. and punished at their discretion, not extending to life or limb.

Sec. 19. " *No free person of color.*" (meaning, I suppose, "no free negro, mulatto, or mestizo ") or slave, can keep, use or employ a still, or other vessel, on his own account, for the distillation of spirituous liquors, or be employed or concerned in vending spirituous liquors of any kind or description, and on conviction thereof, is regarded as guilty of a misdemeanor, and is to be punished not exceeding fifty lashes, at the discretion of the Court; and the still or other vessel is forfeited, and the same is to be sold under an execution to be issued by the Magistrate granting the warrant to apprehend the free negro or slave, and the proceeds of the sale are directed to be paid to the Commissioners of the Poor.

Sec. 20. A slave or free person of color, (meaning as is above suggested) who shall commit a trespass, which would subject a white person to a civil action, and for which no other penalty is prescribed, is regarded as guilty of a misdemeanor, and is to be punished at the discretion of the Court trying him, not extending to life or limb. A

P. L. 497.

P. L. 486, 6th sec. Act of '89.

Acts of '34, p. 12.

The State, ex relatione, Boylston vs. Mag. and freeholders of Marion, Dist. 2 Strob.

Act of 1831, 1st and 2d sec. p. 13.

Act of 31, 4th sec. p. 13.

question will arise under this Act, whether any civil remedy by way
of trespass, can now be had against any negro, mulatto, or mestizo,
for a trespass by him or her committed ?

SEC. 21. A free negro, mulatto, mestizo, or slave, being a distiller, *Act or '31. last
vendor, or retailer of spirituous liquors, who shall sell, exchange, give paragraph, 3d sec.
or otherwise deliver spirituous liquors to a slave, except upon the 11 Stat. 469.
written and express order of the owner, or person having the care of
the slave, shall, upon conviction, (if a slave) be whipped not exceeding fifty lashes ; if a free negro, mulatto, or mestizo, be also whipped
not exceeding fifty lashes, and fined not exceeding $50 ; one half of Act of '44. 11 Stat. 294.
the fine to the informer, the other half to the State.

SEC. 22. A slave, or free person of color, (meaning as before sug- Act of '33, 2d
gested) convicted of a capital offence, is to be punished by hanging ; sec. p. 41.
if convicted of an offence not capital, a slave is to be punished by p. 40.
whipping, confinement in the stocks, or treadmill, or as is prescribed
by the Act of '34, (see ante 1st sec.) imprisonment may be resorted
to. A free negro, mulatto, or mestizo, is liable to the same punishment, *or may be fined.*

SEC. 23. In all parts of the State, (except in Charleston,) slaves Act of '39, sec.
or free persons of color, (meaning as suggested ante 19th sec.) are to 28 and 32. The State vs.
be tried for all offences by a Magistrate and five freeholders ; the Nicholas, Charleston, Jan.
freeholders are to be obtained by the Magistrate, who issues the war- 1848.
rant, summoning eight neighboring freeholders. out of whom the prisoner, (if he be a free negro, mulatto. or mestizo) or the owner or
overseer, (if a slave) may select five to sit upon the trial, and upon
good cause shewn against any freeholder, to be determined by the
Magistrate, another shall be substituted in his place. If the prisoner, the owner, or overseer, should refuse or neglect to make the selection of the five freeholders to sit, the Magistrate may himself make
the selection.

SEC. 24. In Charleston, (including the Parishes of St. Philips and 6th sec. Act of
St. Michael's) slaves, free negroes, mulattoes and mestizoes, are lia- '27. p. 63. 15th sec. Act of
ble to be tried for capital offences by two Judicial Magistrates and '29. p. 30. Act of 1830, sec.
five freeholders, *or slaveholders*, who. I suppose, ought to be obtained 4-5. p. 26. Act of '32. sec.
as directed—ante 22nd section—and in such cases there must be a 1-2. p. 59-60.
concurrence of all of the freeholders, and one of the Magistrates ; in The State vs. Nicholas,
cases not capital, they are to be tried by two Judicial Magistrates Charleston, Jan.
and three freeholders or slaveholders, a concurrence of a majority of 1848.
the jurors and the presiding Magistrate, is enough for conviction ; if
the jurors be unanimous, then in that case the concurrence of the
Magistrate is dispensed with. In all cases, the ministerial Magistrate, issuing the warrant, is to attend the Court, and act as prosecuting officer.

SEC. 25. The anomaly is presented *here* of two different systems of
5

jurisprudence for the State and Charleston.  Both cannot be right, one should give way to the other.

Act of '39, sec.
23, p. 22.  Sec. 26.  The jurors when organized, should be sworn by the Magistrate, to well and truly try the case now pending before you, and adjudge the same according to evidence.  So help you God.

Act of 1754, sec.
4.  7 Stat. 427.
Act of '39, sec.
28, p. 22.  Sec. 27.  A slave, free negro, mulatto or mestizo, charged with a criminal offence, is to be tried within six days. if it be practicable to give at least one day's notice of the time and place of trial to the free negro, mulatto, mestizo, the owner, overseer, or other person having the care and government of the slave—*which notice must, in all cases, be fairly given before the trial can proceed.*

Act of '39, p. 22.  Sec. 28.  On the trial of a slave, free negro, mulatto. or mestizo, it is the duty of the Magistrate to state in writing, plainly and distinctly, the offence charged against the prisoner, and for which he is on trial; to this charge the prisoner ought to be required to answer: either by himself, or through his guardian, master, owner, overseer, or other person having the care and government of such slave on trial, or by the attorney employed to defend such prisoner.  In every such trial, the prisoner is entitled to the benefit of the services of an attorney at law, to defend him.  The Magistrate is bound to keep a correct statement of the testimony given against and for the prisoner, and to annex it to *the charge,* (the accusation.)  The judgment of the Court in the country Districts and Parishes. must be in writing. and signed by the Magistrate and any four of the freeholders, or by the whole, if they agree.  In Charleston, it must be made up as directed, (ante sec. 23.) and must be signed by those required to concur in it.  It is in all parts of the State to be returned to the Clerk's office of each judicial district, and be there filed.

Act of '33, sec. 3.
p. 41.
Act of '39, sec.
28, p. 23.  Sec. 29.  When a slave, free negro, mulatto or mestizo. is capitally convicted, an application may be made to any one of the Judges of the Courts of Law of this State, in open Court, or at Chambers. for a new trial.  The Magistrate presiding, is required for such purpose: to furnish a full report of the trial ; and if from that, as well as from affidavits on the part of the prisoner, (which before being laid before the Judge must be shewn to the Magistrate presiding.) the Judge should be satisfied the conviction is erroneous, a new trial is to be ordered, on which neither the Magistrate, nor Magistrates, nor any of the freeholders, who before sat on the case, are to sit again.  To afford opportunity for this appeal to be made, or for an application to the Governor for a pardon, time, reasonable time, must be allowed by the Court between the conviction and the execution of the sentence.

Sec. 30.  Under these provisions, there is not any very well settled practice.  Before a motion for new trial ought to be heard, reasonable notice of the time and place of such motion should be given to the

Magistrate presiding. When a new trial is ordered, I have always directed the Clerk of the Court to summon the Magistrate and free-holders, who should try the case *de novo*, and to give notice to all concerned, of the time and place of trial, and if necessary, to issue summons for the witnesses. This seemed to secure, in the best way I could devise, consistently with the law, an impartial administration of it.

SEC. 31. The right of appeal, in cases not capital, and to afford sufficient time in such cases, for an application for pardon, ought to be provided for. For many are the errors and abuses of power committed in this behalf. The whippings inflicted by the sentence of Courts trying slaves and free negroes, are most enormous—utterly disproportioned to offences, and should be prevented by all the means in our power. In all cases where whipping is to be resorted to, I would limit the punishment by law, in all cases affecting both black and white, to forty, save one, and direct it to be inflicted in portions, and at considerable intervals of time. Thus mingling imprisonment and whipping together, and holding the rod suspended, in the contemplation of the party, until the delay itself would be worse punishment than the infliction.

SEC. 32. The tribunal for the trial of slaves and free negroes, (a Magistrate and freeholders of the vicinage) is the worst system which could be devised. The consequence is, that the passions and prejudices of the neighborhood, arising from a recent offence, enter into the trial, and often lead to the condemnation of the innocent.— The Charleston scheme is better than that which prevails in the country. Still I think it none of the best. I would establish a tribunal to consist of one judicial Magistrate, to be appointed by the Legislature, to try all criminal cases against free negroes, mulattoes, mestizoes or slaves. He should be compelled to hold his Court on the first Wednesday in every month, at the Court House; and he should have the power to direct a Constable, (whom he should be authorized to appoint to attend his Courts) to summon 24 freeholders or slaveholders of the District, and out of them a jury of 12 should be empannelled to try the prisoner, allowing him as far as ten, a peremptory challenge, and on cause shewn, to the balance of the pannel. The Magistrate issuing the warrant, should be required to state the offence and act as prosecuting officer. To the charge thus presented, the prisoner should be required to answer; and he should have the benefit of an attorney's services, to defend him, on the law and evidence. The judicial Magistrate should be required to charge the jury on the law and the facts, as a Judge of the Law Courts now does. The jury should simply say guilty or not guilty. The Magistrate presiding, should pronounce the judgment of the law. The prisoner on conviction should have the right of appeal to the Court of Appeals, and no sentence should be passed until the case was there heard, and the prisoner remanded for judgment. The judicial Magistrate, his Constable, and the Magistrate issuing the warrant, should be compensated by fees. to be paid, in all cases. by the State.

Act of '29, p. 28, sec. 1.

SEC. 33. Under the law. as it now stands, the State is liable for all the costs attending negro trials. (except free negroes. mulattoes, and mestizoes, in the Parishes of St. Philips, and St. Michael's, who if convicted, and able to pay. are declared liable to pay the same, and

P. L. 168.

also under the 21st section of the Act of 1740: if the prosecution against a slave, free negro, mulatto, or mestizo. appears to be malicious, the Court trying the case. and satisfied of that fact, may order and compel the prosecutor to pay the costs.) This provision of the

Acts of '29, p. 28, sec. 2.

21st section of the Act of 1740, is re-enacted, as to slaves, in the Magistrates' and Constables' Acts for St. Philip's and St. Michael's, passed in 1829.

Exparte Brown, 2d hall, 323.

SEC. 34. A slave cannot be twice tried, and punished, for the same offence.

SEC. 35. If a slave be out of the house or plantation, where such

5th sec. Act 1740.
P. L. 165.

slave resides, or without some white person in company, and should refuse to submit to, and undergo the examination of any white person, it is lawful for such white person to pursue, apprehend. and moderately correct such slave, and if such slave shall assault and strike such white person, *such slave may be lawfully killed.*

SEC. 36. Masters, overseers, or other persons, have the power to apprehend and take up any slave found out of his or her master's or owner's plantation at any time, but more especially on Saturday

Sec. 36, Act of 1740.
P. L. 172.

nights or Sundays, or other holidays, not being on lawful business, or not with a ticket from the master, or not having some white person in company, and even with a ticket, if armed with wooden swords or other mischievous and dangerous weapons, and to disarm such slave, and all such mentioned in this section, to whip.

35th sec. of the Act of 1740.
P. L. 169. 1st sec.
Act of '88.
P. L. 441.
63d sec. Act of 11 Stat. 16.

SEC. 37. Any person is authorized to take up any runaway slave, and it seems. it is now the duty of the person taking up a runaway, (when he knows, or can be informed without difficulty, to whom such slave belongs) to send such slave to the said owner. but if the owner

13th sec. Ordinance of the city of Charleston.
39 City Laws, 315.

be unknown. then in Charleston District, it is the duty of the person taking up such runaway slave to send within five days, the same to the Work House in the city of Charleston. the master of the Work House is to admit every such slave upon a certificate from a Magistrate of the District, or Mayor, or one of the Aldermen of the city, containing the particulars of the apprehension of such fugitive slave, and requiring his confinement; in all other parts of the State the runaway slave is to be sent to the Gaol of the District. It is the duty of the Master, Gaoler or Sheriff, to securely keep the slave so committed, and if the same escape by negligence, the Master or Sheriff, (for the gaoler is merely the Sheriff's keeper,) is liable to the owner

for the value of the slave. or such damages as may be sustained by such escape. Information of the slave so committed to the care of the Master of the Work House, is to be by him sent to the owner. if known; if he be unknown, the Master of the Work House is to advertise such slave in the city paper. (under the advice of the City Att'y.) giving the name, age, and other further description, so that the owner may be informed the slave is in custody. In other parts of the State, the runaway is to be advertised once a week for 3 months, in some public gazette, by the Sheriff or Gaoler, who is also required, if the owner's name and address can be obtained, to give him specific notice of the confinement of the said runaway. The advertisement must contain the name, age, and other particular description of such slave, and the name of the person said to be the owner. The Gaoler or Sheriff, and the Master of the Work House, is liable to a fine of 10s. or $2 14 for such slave committed as a runaway, neglected to be advertised. The runaway is to be kept for 12 months, if not claimed by the owner, and in Charleston, proof of property made on oath before one of the Judges of the Common Pleas, or any Magistrate, within twelve months from the date of the advertisement in Charleston, in other parts of the State, from the commitment. the runaway is to be sold. In Charleston the sale is to be made by the City Sheriff, he giving one month's notice of the time, place, and reason of such sale; he is to give to the purchaser a receipt for the money arising from such sale, specifying the reasons of the sale, and he (the City Sheriff) is directed to pay the said proceeds to the City Treasury. Out of the fund so paid over. is to be deducted the expenses of the said runaway. as provided and allowed by law. The balance is to be retained by the City Treasurer, for the owner, but if not claimed within a year and a day it is to be paid into the State Treasury, and out of it. I presume, the Commissioners of Public Buildings of Charleston District are entitled to draw it. under the general law of '39. In other parts of the State, the Sheriff of the District is to advertise the runaway for a month, and then to sell ; and after paying the charges or expenses allowed by law, the balance is to be paid to the Commissioners of Public Buildings, and is to belong to them absolutely. if not claimed by the owner of the slave so runaway. within two years. The title to be executed by the Sheriff to the purchaser of such runaway, is good, and bars the rights of the owner. Any neglect or default in the duties required by the 53d section of the Act of '39, subjects a Gaoler or Sheriff to an action on the case.

SEC. 38. A person taking up a runaway, and failing to send the same to the work house, or the District gaol within five days, is liable to pay 20s. or $4 28-100 for every day the same may be retained. The person taking up a runaway. is entitled to 10s. or $2 14-100 for taking up such runaway, 4d. or 7-100 for every mile from the place where taken to the owner's residence, (if the runaway be carried to the owner,) or to the district gaol or the work house, and half a dollar per day for the travel, computing the journey at 25 miles to the day. To entitle the person taking up a runaway, to these allowances, he must carry the slave to a neighboring Magistrate, who may examine on oath the captor, touching the time and distance he has necessarily travelled, and shall go with such slave, and the said Magistrate shall give a certificate on a just estimate of such time and distance, and on presenting such certificate, the gaoler is to give his note for the same payable to the bearer. The Master of the Work House is to pay the same, instead of giving a note. These fees are to be paid to the Gaoler, or Master of the Work House, by the owner, or out of the sale of the said runaway, if he should not be claimed by the owner and be sold.

36th and 37th sec. of the Act of 1740.
P. L. 169.

11 Stat. 11.

SEC. 39. It is the duty of the Master of the Work House, Gaoler, or Sheriff, to provide sufficient food, drink, clothing and covering, for every runaway slave delivered into the custody of either. The Gaoler or Sheriff is entitled to charge 20 cents per day for each runaway confined, and also for all necessary expenses in providing clothes or blankets. In the Work House, a runaway slave is directed to be put to labor on the tread-mill, and therefore no charge for diet is made.

20th sec. Ord. of '39, City Laws, 315.

SEC. 40. Each militia beat company, by its commander, (except the company or companies on Charleston Neck.) is divided into convenient patrol districts. All the free white male inhabitants, above the age of eighteen years, of each patrol district, are liable to do patrol duty, except aliens or transient persons above the age of forty-five years, or who have not resided within the State for six months, or persons who are above the age of forty-five, who do not own slaves, or alien enemies. Persons liable to do patrol duty, may send in their places, respectively, an able-bodied white man, between the ages of sixteen and sixty, as a substitute; and for failing to discharge patrol duty, in person or by substitute, each person liable to do the same, without a legal excuse, is liable to pay a fine of $2 for each default, and ten per cent. on his general tax of the preceding year.

1st, 2d, and 3d sec. Act of '39.
11 Stat. 58.

3d and 4th sec. Act of '39.
11 Stat. 58.

SEC. 41. It is the duty of the commanding officer of each beat company, to make out a roll of the inhabitants of each patrol division, liable to do patrol duty, and from such roll, at each regular muster of his company, to prick off, *at his discretion*, any number of persons to do patrol duty until the next muster, and appoint *some prudent and discreet person* to command the said patrol. If the officer commanding the beat company, fails to prick off, at each muster, the patrol of each division, or the commandant of the patrol fails in his duty, each of them is liable to a fine not exceeding $30.

SEC. 42. It is the duty of the commandant of the patrol to call 5th and 13 h sec.
them out at least once a fortnight, and to take up, and correct with Act of '39.
11 Stat. 58—60.
stripes, not exceeding 20, with a switch or cowskin, all slaves found
outside of their owner's or employer's plantation, without a ticket or
letter to shew the reasonableness of his absence, or some white person in company to give an account of the business of such slave;
and also, if the slave have a ticket, and has in his possession, a gun,
pistol or other offensive weapon, unless such slave be on lawful business, or in company with some white person not less than ten years
of age. Fire arms, and other offensive weapons, found by the patrol Act of '43,
in the possession of a slave, in violation of the above provisions, are 11 Stat. 252.
liable to seizure by them, and condemnation and forfeiture to the use
of the regiment to which the patrol may belong. To obtain such
forfeiture, the leader of the patrol making the seizure, must, within
ten days, go before the nearest Magistrate, and make oath of the
manner, time and place of taking; and if the Magistrate shall be satisfied of the legality of the seizure, he shall summon the owner of
the slave from whom the arms have been taken, to appear before
him within ten days, to shew cause why the arms should not be con-
demoed. If the owner should fail to appear, or appearing, should
shew insufficient cause, the said arms or weapons shall, by certificate
under the hand of the Magistrate, be "*declared condemned*," and
may be sold within ten days, and the proceeds, after payment of the
costs, paid to the paymaster of the regiment.

SEC. 43. The patrol have the power, and are required to enter into 6th sec Act of '39,
any disorderly house, vessel or boat, suspected of harboring, traffick- p. 59. 11 Stat.
ing or dealing with negroes, whether the same be occupied by white
persons, free negroes, mulattoes, mestizoes or slaves; and to apprehend and correct all slaves found there, by whipping, (unless, as I
apprehend, such slaves shall have not only a ticket to be absent, but
also a ticket to trade.) The patrol is required to inform a Magistrate of such white persons, free negroes, mulattoes or mestizoes, as
may be found in such house, vessel or boat, and to detain, until recovered by law, such produce or articles for trafficking, as may be
therein found, if such detention be authorized by any three freeholders or any Magistrate. It is the duty of the owner of each boat or
vessel navigating the public rivers or canals of this State, to keep
and produce to the Magistrates or patrols, when required, a list of all
the negroes composing the crew, with their owners' names, and a description of their persons.

SEC. 44. The patrol may, as is stated in the 44th and 45th sec- 11th and 14th
tions of chapter 2nd of this digest. break up unlawful assemblies of sec Act of '39,
11 Stat. 59, 60,
slaves, and inflict punishment on slaves there found, not exceeding 61.
20 stripes, with a switch or cowskin.

SEC. 45. Every owner of a settled plantation, who does not live on the same six months in every year, and who employs upon the same fifteen or more slaves. is required to keep upon the same, some white man, capable of performing patrol duty, under a penalty of fifty cents per month for each and every working slave employed on the said plantation.

SEC. 46. Patrols are not liable, in the discharge of their duty, to the payment of any tolls.

SEC. 47. In incorporated towns and villages, the power and duty of regulating the patrol in the same, is vested in and devolved upon the municipal authorities of the same.

SEC. 48. The Captain of a Beat Company, cannot constitute himself the Captain of a Patrol.

SEC. 49. The ticket or pass to a slave, need not state the place to which he or she is to go. and a patrol whipping a slave, with such a pass. are trespassers. The form given in the Act of 1740, " Permit this slave to be absent from the plantation of A. B. until ———;" or any other equivalent form, will be sufficient.

SEC. 50. It is the duty of Captains or Commanders of Patrol. to keep their respective commands in good order and demeanor, when on duty ; and any patrol man misbehaving himself or neglecting or disobeying the orders of his commandant, is liable to a fine of not less than $2, nor more than $20. If the Captain of a Patrol acts disorderly, so as to defeat the proper execution of the patrol laws, he is liable to be returned by any member of his command, or any other person competent to give evidence, to the commanding officer of the Beat Company, who is to return him to a Court Martial for trial, and if found guilty. he may be fined not less than $5, nor more than $50.

SEC. 51. Each Captain of the Patrol is required, at the net regular muster of the Beat Company, after his appointment. to make a return, on oath, of the performance of his duties. Failing to make such return. he is liable to a fine of $20

SEC. 52. The penalties to be incurred by the commanding officers of Beat Companies, commandants of the patrols. and patrol men, for neglect of duty, or violation of law, may be imposed by Courts Martial.

SEC. 53. If the patrol be sued, and the party suing. fail to recover, he is liable to treble costs ; which is full costs, to which is added one half, and then half of that half.

SEC. 54. The Act of '39 in repealing all other laws on the subject of the patrol, *unfortunately* excepts the Act regulating the performance of patrol. duty on Charleston Neck. The Act of '23. so saved from repeal, differs in many respects from the general law, which it is now necessary to state. 1st. A majority of the company officers is to direct how the company is to be divided into patrol districts, and the Captain is so to divide it, and it is so to continue until altered by a majority of said officers. The officers failing to do this duty, are liable to a fine of $30, to be recovered in the Court of Law. (by indictment) as no mode is appointed by the Act.  2d. All *2d section.* white males above 18 and under 60, residing in said patrol districts, (except ministers of the Gospel) all females owning ten slaves above the age of ten years, and *all persons* having settled farms, or a house and lot, with five or more slaves above the age of 16, residing within the said *companies,* are liable to do patrol duty. Females required to do patrol duty, must of course do so by substitute.  3d. The commanding officer, or officers of a company are to appoint *in writing,* *3d section.* the leader of the patrol, whose qualification and term of office is the same as pointed out in section 40. The person so appointed refusing to accept, the commanding officer or officers of companies or the leaders of patrol, not performing the duties required, are liable to a fine of $20, to be recovered by indictment, in the Court of Law, and paid to the Commissioners of Cross Roads. No person can be compelled to serve as leader, more than once in 12 months. 4th. The patrol is not only authorized to enter disorderly houses, &c., as stated in section *5th section.* 42; but if resisted, they are authorized to break open doors, windows, and locks; they are required to produce to the Magistrate, whom they may inform of white persons, free negroes, mulattoes and mestizoes, found in such houses, the produce or articles for trafficking found there, *to be disposed of according to law.* 5th. The leader of a patrol is, as is stated in section 49, to keep his command in good order, &c.; *6th and 7th sec-* any patrol man, misbehaving, &c., is liable to a fine of $2, to *be tion.* imposed by the officers of the company to which he belongs, and to be paid to the Commissioners of Cross Roads, Charleston Neck.— A leader acting disorderly may be proceeded against as stated in section 49; he is to be tried by a Court consisting of the officers of his company, or any 3 officers of the Regiment, and may be fined $10, to be paid to the same authorities. Commissioners of Cross Roads, Charleston Neck. 6th. A substitute for patrol must be between 18 *8th section.* and 60. 7th. Free negroes, mulattoes, or mestizoes, found on *10th section.* Charleston Neck, are to be treated by the patrol, as slaves, unless they produce their free papers, office copies, or other satisfactory evidence of freedom. If found out of their own houses, or the enclosure of their employer, not having a regular ticket from their guardian, after 9 P. M., from 20th Sept. to 20th March, and 10 P. M., from 20th March to 20th Sept. they are declared liable to be treated as slaves without a pass. 8th. No grocery, retail shop, or any store, shop, or place, wherein are vended spirituous liquors, is to be kept open on the *11th section.* Sabbath day, or any other day after 9 P. M., from 20th Sept. to 20th March; and after 10 P. M., from 20th March to 20th Sept., any owner, or occupant violating this law, or trading, trafficking, or bartering therein, with any slaves, free negroes, mulattoes, or mestizoes, is

6

liable to a fine of $50, to be recovered by indictment, in the Court of Law, and paid to the Commissioners of Cross Roads, Charleston

12th section. Neck. 9th. Each inhabitant of Charleston Neck. liable to patrol duty, is required to provide and carry with him on service, a good gun or pistol, in order, with at least 6 ball cartridges for the same, or cutlass, under the penalty of $2, and 10 per cent on his general tax of

13th section. the year preceding. 10th. The commanding officer of the company or companies on Charleston Neck, may appoint a Secretary, whose duty it shall be to prepare and lay before the Military Courts herein

14th section. before mentioned. all necessary papers, and to keep a record of the proceedings of the same, which is to be open to the inspection of all interested. For this duty, he is exempted from patrol duty. 11th.

15th section. The leader of each patrol may appoint a warner to summon the patrol ; and for this duty he is exempted from the patrol. 12th. It is the duty of the officers commanding the companies on Charleston

16th section. Neck, and all Magistrates, to inform the leaders of the patrols. of unlawful assemblies, of negroes, (slaves.) free negroes. mulattoes, and mestizoes. The leaders on receipt of this information. are to turn out their patrols, and discharge the duty required by law ; failing to do this, they are respectively liable to a fine of $20, to be paid to the Commissioners of Cross Roads. Charleston Neck. For uniformity sake, I think this Act of '23. should be repealed.

Act of '45, 1st
and 2d sec.
11 Stat. 344. SEC. 55. The Commissioners of Cross Roads on Charleston Neck, by the Act of '45. were authorized to build a Guard House. and it provides that all free negroes, mulattoes, mestizoes, and slaves, on Charleston Neck, charged or found guilty of violating the law, shall be therein confined, and *there* punished ; and also slaves, free negroes, mulattoes, and mestizoes, taken up by the patrol, shall there be whipped according to the patrol law, unless the owner or person having charge of such slaves, free negroes, mulattoes. or mestizoes. or their guardians, shall pay to the Commissioners of Cross Roads, one dollar for each of said slaves, free negroes, mulattoes or mestizoes.

## CHAPTER IV.

*The Rights—Civil and Criminal Remedies—And Liabilities of the Master. Also the Law to Prevent the Disturbance of the Peace in relation to Slaves and Free Negroes.*

Sec. 1. The right of a master in a slave, and all which appertains or belongs to him. is that of property. If the slave be in the possession of another, his owner may maintain detinue for his specific delivery, or may have a bill in Equity, to compel his possession to be restored, (unless he may have been bought for sale, in which case the owner is left to his remedy at law.) or may bring trover to recover the damages sustained in his conversion. The owner may bring Sarter vs. Gordon. 2d Hill C.<br>R. 121.
trespass for any forcible taking of the slave from his possession, or for any forcible injury done to his person. So too. if a slave wander from the possession of the owner, and another employ him, the owner may bring assumpsit for his labor, or trover for the time he may be in the employment of a third person. or if such person *knew he was a slave*, the action on the case might be sustained. So too. if a bailee Bell vs. Lakin,<br>1 McMull. 364,<br>370—2.
abuse or employ a slave differently from the contract of bailment, and he is killed or injured, the bailee would be liable to the owner.— So too, a common carrier transporting a slave from one place to another, is liable for an injury to, the death, or loss of the slave, as he Helton vs. Caston. 2d Bail, 95.<br>Duncan vs. Rail Road Co. 2d<br>Rich. 613.<br>Clark ads. McDonald, 4 McC.<br>233.
would be for other articles, with this exception, if he shews that he used proper care and diligence. and the injury, loss, or death, resulted from the act of the slave, then he would not be liable. Any employment of a slave, without the consent of the master, by which the slave is killed. or injured. makes the person so employing him, liable for the damages sustained by the owner. For personal property, in the possession of the slave, and commonly called the property of the slave, the master may maintain the same actions against one possessing himself of it, as he could for the slave himself. For harboring a runaway slave, knowing him to be such, an action on the case can be maintained by the owner. Wright vs. Gray,<br>2d Bay, 464.

Sec. 2. A contract for the hire of a slave for a year is an entire contract. yet if the slave die, his wages will be apportioned. But if the slave be sick, or runaway. no deduction is to be made on either account. The owner is not liable generally, for medical services rendered to his slave, while in the possession of one to whom he may be hired. The master is liable for medical services rendered to his slave without his knowledge, if the slave be in great danger. Pace vs. Parnell, 2d Bail.424.<br>Wells vs. Kenerly, 4 McC.<br>123.<br>Johnston vs.<br>Barrett, 2d Bail.<br>362.

Sec. 3. By the 5th section of the Act of '39, provision is made, if any white man shall beat or abuse any slave, quietly and peaceably being in his master's plantation, or found any where without the same. with a lawful ticket, that he shall forfeit $50, to be recovered by and to the use of the owner, by action of debt, besides being liable 5th sec. Act of<br>'39. 11 Stat. 58.

Caldwell et. al.
ads. Langford, 1
McMull. 275.

to the owner, in an action of trespass for damages. Under this provision, it has been held, that where a slave was found out of his master's plantation, but had a ticket, and was whipped by the party finding him, that the master could maintain the action under the Act, and recover.

Acts of 1823, p.
64.

SEC. 4. The Act of '23, for the regulation of patrol duty on Charleston Neck, section 4, provides if any white man shall *wantonly* beat, or abuse any slave, quietly and peaceably being in his or her owner's enclosure, or found anywhere without the same, with a lawful ticket, he shall forfeit $50, to be recovered by the owner, and to his use, besides being liable to the owner in an action of trespass for damages. This provision is identical with that of '39, except that in the Act of '23, the beating or abusing must be *wantonly*. In the Act of '39, no such word is used. It may be under the Act of '23, malice, or cruelty, would have to be shewn.

3d sec. Act of
1747. P. L. 215.

SEC. 5. The 3rd section of the Act of 1747, provides, that if any overseer or manager shall employ upon his own account or business, any of the negroes committed to his care, by sending them on errands, or in any other manner whatever, such overseer or manager shall pay the sum of 10s. (equal to $2 14-100,) for every day he or they shall so employ any negro committed to the care of such overseer or mana

1st section.

ger. (This penalty, another part of the Act, section 1st, directs to be recovered before a Justice of the Peace, Magistrate now, in the manner and form prescribed for the recovery of small debts and damages.) The 3rd section further provides, that to establish the fact

Last paragraph
3d section.

of the employment of the owner's slaves by the overseer or manager, *the information of the negroes* shall be sufficient, unles *the overseer or manager* will exculpate himself on oath.

1 McMull. Rep.
480.

In the case of Dillard vs. Wallace, I ruled that this provision was obsolete from non-user. The Court of Appeals, admitting that its enforcement had been hitherto unknown, and ninety years had then elapsed from its enactment. held that it was still not obsolete. It is therefore a law, however anomalous in its provision about evidence, still to be enforced.

6th sec. Act of
1740. P. L. 165.

SEC. 6. If any slave shall be beat, bruised, maimed or disabled, in the lawful business or service of his master, owner, overseer or other person having charge of such slave, by any person or persons, not having sufficient cause or authority, (of which cause the Magistrate trying the case is to judge.) he or they shall forfeit 40s. current money, equal to 5s. 8d. sterling, or $1 20-100. to the use of the poor of the District or Parish. If the slave or slaves be maimed or disabled from performing his or her or their work, the person or persons beating the slave, shall also forfeit and pay to the owner, 15s. current money, equal to about 44 cents, for every day he may be unable to discharge his usual service, and the charge of the cure of such slave.

If the damages in the whole do not exceed £20 current money, equal to $12 27-100. they, as also the penalty for the use of the poor. may be recovered before a Magistrate ; and if the offender shall produce no goods on which the same may be levied, the Magistrate is authorized to commit him to gaol until the same be paid.

These provisions have been very little noticed, and furnish so poor a relief for the abuse to which they apply, that they will rarely be resorted to. The action of trespass is an abundantly better remedy. Still. this law exists. and may. in the case described in the Act, be resorted to by owners, if they choose so to do. They cannot, however. have this remedy, and also an action of trespass.

Sec. 7. Any person who shall give a ticket or written permit to a slave, the property of or under the charge of another, (without the *Acts of '35, p. 83.* consent, or against the will of such owner, or person having charge,) authorizing such slave to be absent, or to deal, trade or traffic, such person is liable to be indicted, and on conviction, to be punished by fine not exceeding $1000, and imprisonment not exceeding 12 months.

Notwithstanding this Act, a person who might give a ticket to a *The State vs.* slave, with a view to aid a slave in running away and departing from *Blease,1 McMull.* his master's service, might be tried and capitally convicted under the *472.* Act of 1754.

Sec. 8. If a white person *harbor, conceal or entertain* any runaway or fugitive slave. he or she is liable to be indicted for a misdemea- *Acts of '21. p. 20.* nor, or prosecuted in a civil action for damages, at the election of the owner or person injured. If indicted and convicted, the offender is liable to a fine not exceeding $1000, and imprisonment not exceeding 12 months. The owner may proceed by indictment, and also civilly. *The State vs.* at the same time, he cannot be put to his election until the trial. *Stein, 1 Rich.* *189.*

Sec. 9. If a person be maimed, wounded or disabled. in pursuing, *8th sec. Act of* apprehending or taking any slave that is run away, or charged with *1740.  P. L. 165.* any criminal offence, or in doing any thing else, in obedience to the Act of 1740, he shall receive such reward from the public as the General Assembly may think fit; and if he be killed, his heirs, executors or administrators shall receive the same.

I do not know that any claim has ever been made under this law. Still, however, it seems to be of force, and a claimant would be entitled to the benefit of its provisions.

Sec. 10. The Court trying and capitally convicting a slave, is to appraise the same, not exceeding $200, and certify such appraisement *Act of '43. 1st* to the Treasurer of the Division within which the slave may be con- *sec. 11 Stat. 264.* demned ; and in the event of the slave being executed, in pursuance of the sentence, the Treasurer is directed to pay the appraisement to the owner.

Sec. 11. If a white person game with a free negro, mulatto or mestizo, or slave, or shall bet upon any game played, wherein one of *Act of 1834. 6th* *sec. 7 Stat. 469.*

The State vs.
Nates, 3d Hill,
200.
the parties is a free negro, mulatto, mestizo or slave, or shall be willingly present, aiding and abetting, where any game of chance is played, as aforesaid, in such case; such white person, upon conviction by indictment, is liable to receive 39 lashes, and to be fined and imprisoned at the discretion of the Court; one half of the fine is to go

Act of '44, 11
Stat. 291.
to the informer, the other half to the State.

SEC. 12. Any shop-keeper, trader or other person, by himself or
1st sec. Act of
'47.  7 Stat. 451.
any other person acting for him or her, who shall buy or purchase from any slave, in any part of this State, any corn, rice, peas, or other grain, bacon, flour, tobacco, indigo, cotton, blades, hay, or any other article whatsoever, or shall otherwise deal, trade or traffic with any slave not having a permit so to deal, trade or traffic, or, to sell any such article, from or under the hand of his master or owner, or such other person as may have the care and management of such slave, upon conviction, is liable to be fined not exceeding $1000, and to be
2d section.
imprisoned not more than 12 months, nor less than 1 month. It is the business of the party trading with a slave, to produce and prove the permit.

SEC. 13. If a slave enter a shop, store, or house of any kind, used
5th sec. Act of
'34.  7 Stat. 469.
State vs. Stone,
Rice's Rep. 147.
for dealing, trading and trafficking, with an article, and come out without the same, or enter without an article, and come out with one, it is sufficient evidence to convict the owner or person occupying the same for trade, in an indictment under the Act of 1817.

SEC. 14. If a white person, being a distiller, vendor or retailer of
3d sec. Act of
'34.  7 Stat. 469.
spirituous liquors, shall sell, exchange, give, or in any otherwise deliver any spirituous liquors to any slave, except upon the written and express order of the owner or person having the care and management of the slave, he shall, upon conviction, be fined not exceeding $100, and imprisoned not exceeding six months; one half of the said
Act of '44, 11
Stat. 294.
fine to the use of the informer, and the other half to the use of the State.

SEC. 15. One effect resulting from the Act, and certainly neither
The State vs.
Evans, 3d Hill,
191.
intended nor anticipated by the Legislature, was to repeal the penalty of the Act of 1817, quoad distillers, vendors and retailers, (the very persons who, above all others, ought to bear the heaviest pen-
The State vs.
Stone, Rice's
Rep. 147.
alties,) in relation to the sale or exchange of spirituous liquors. The rule of evidence established by the Act of 1817, as to the production and proof of the permit, still remains in force.

SEC. 16. In an indictment for trading with a slave, or giving or
The State vs.
Schroder, 3d
Hill, 61
delivering spirituous liquors to a slave, it is necessary that the slave should be described, when possible, by his own and his owner's name, or if that be not possible, by some equivalent description of the slave.

SEC. 17. In indictments under the Act of 1834, although the rule
The State vs.
Avulls, 2d Strob
of evidence established by its 5th section does not apply, and so, too, under the Act of 1817, where the trading is not in "a shop, store, or

house of any kind, used for trading " yet if the slave be seen to enter with an article, and come out without it, or to enter without an article, and come out with one, it is a fact, from which, at common law, a presumption may arise of guilt, and on which the jury may convict.

SEC. 18. It was decided immediately after the passage of the Act of 1817, that the sale to a slave, *of any article whatsoever*, or purchase from a slave of any *article whatsoever*, belonging to the slave, his master, or any other person, was a violation of the law.

SEC. 19. If the master, or overseer, or other person having charge of the slave, send a slave with goods to detect another, in dealing trading or trafficking with a slave, and stand by, and see the trading, it does not excuse the defendant, he still is guilty.

SEC. 20. If the owner, or overseer, or other person having charge of the slave, go with him to make the sale or purchase, and stand by and assent to the same, the vendor would not be guilty. For then, the trading might be regarded as that of the master by his slave.

SEC. 21. If the trader be in the habit of trading with slaves, and had authorized his clerk so to trade, he may be convicted for a trading with a slave, by his clerk in his absence. But the principal cannot be criminally answerable for the act of his clerk, unless done with his knowledge and consent actual, or implied. The same rule holds as to a partner.

SEC. 22. An overseer trading with his employer's slaves, may be indicted and convicted, under the Act of 1817.

SEC. 23. Before the Act of '34, a person who sold liquor to a slave might be indicted for trading with a slave without a ticket, and also for retailing. It follows, since the Act of '34 is substituted for that of '17, so far as the penalty is concerned, that a person now may be indicted for selling, giving, exchanging or delivering spirituous liquors to a slave, and for retailing without a license, although there be but one sale and delivery.

SEC. 24. If one sell spirituous liquor to a slave, or to another for him, without a permit from his owner, employer, or other person having charge of him, and the slave die in consequence of the too free use of the liquor so sold, the person so selling, is liable, in an action on the case, for the value of the slave to the owner.

SEC. 25. A license to retail, cannot be granted to an applicant, unless he will swear that he will not, during his license, sell, give, exchange, barter or otherwise deliver spirituous liquors to any slave contrary to the law on that subject. If he has been engaged before in the business, he must also swear, that he has not during his past license, sold, given, delivered, exchanged, bartered, or otherwise delivered spirituous liquors to a slave contrary to law.

SEC. 26. If a master or other person having charge of a slave who may be accused of any capital or other crime, shall conceal or convey

The State vs. Suber. Fall Ter y 1844.
The State vs. Von Glous. I McMull. 1-7.
The State vs. Anone. 2 N. and McC. 27.

The State vs. Stroud, 2 N. and McC. 34 Note.
The State vs. Anone. 2 N. and McC. 27.

The State vs Coleman. (not reported.)
The State vs. Isaacs, 1 Speers, 224.

The State vs. Anne. 2 N. and McC. 27.
The State vs. Matthiew, decided at Columbia, May '35.
The State vs. Coleman, Dud. 32.
The State vs. Chandler, 2 Strob.

The State vs. Sonnerkalb. 2 N. and McC 280.
The State vs. O'Sullivan, at Nisi Prius.

Harrison vs. Berkley, 1 Strob. 525.

4th section Act of '34, 11 Stat. p. 469.

20th sec. Act of 1740. P. L. 165.

away such slave, so he cannot be brought to trial and punishment,
such master or other person shall be liable to forfeit £250 current
money, equal to £35 16s. 5d. or $153 58-100, if the crime be capital;
if not capital, then the forfeiture is £50 currency, equal to £7 3s. 3d.
or $30 70. This provision, in capital felonies, supersedes the com-
mon law offence of accessory, after the fact in a crime committed by
a slave, so far as owners and other persons having charge of a slave
may be concerned.

The State vs.
McAliley, Col'a.
May 1840.

SEC. 27. A master is liable for the acts of his slave, done negligently, unskilfully, or wilfully, in the course of any public employment or business carried on by him, under the authority or with the
consent of his master. *As where*, a slave navigating his master's
vessel, so *negligently* managed his craft as to injure a wharf; or to run
down a car of fish, or where a slave carpenter, with his master's
assent, actual or implied, undertakes to repair a house, and in doing
it, does it so *unskilfully*, that the whole building falls down, or where
a slave blacksmith, in shoeing a horse, becomes enraged with him,
and *wilfully* knocks out the horse's eye with his shoeing hammer, in
all these cases, the master is liable, according to the principles which
I have above stated.

Drayton ads.
Moore. Parker
vs. Gordon, Dud.
268.
O'Connell vs.
S rong. Dud.
264.
Snee vs. Trice, 1
Brev. 178.

SEC. 28· The master is not liable for the unauthorized acts of his
slave, done without his knowledge or consent, actual or implied, and
not in any public business or employment, in which he has placed his
slave.

Snee vs. Trice, 2
Bay 345.
Wingis vs.
Smith. 3 McC.
400.

SEC. 29. Any person or persons, who shall, on his, her, or their own
behalf, or under color, or in virtue of any commission, or authority
from any State or public authority of any State in this Union, or any
foreign power, come within this State, with the intent to disturb, hin-
der, or counteract the operation of laws made or to be made, in relation to slaves, free negroes, mulattoes, and mestizoes, are liable to be
arrested, and if not bailed, committed to gaol by any of the Judges of
this State, including the Recorder, for a high misdemeanor, and on
conviction is liable to be sentenced to banishment from the State, and
to be fined and imprisoned at the discretion of the Court.

1st sec. Act '44.
11 Stat. 292.

SEC. 30. Any person within this State, who shall at any time
accept any commission or authority from any State, or public authority of any State in this Union, or from any foreign
power, in relation to slaves or free persons of color, and who
shall commit any overt act with an intent to disturb the peace
or security of this State. or with intent to disturb, counteract, or hin-
der the laws of this State, made or to be made, in relation to slaves
or free negroes, mulattoes, or mestizoes, shall be deemed guilty of a
misdemeanor, and upon conviction thereof, shall be sentenced to pay
for the first offence, a fine not exceeding $1000, and to be imprisoned
not exceeding one year; and for the second offence, he shall be

2nd sec. Act of
'44. 11 Stat. 292

imprisoned 7 years, and pay a fine not less than $1000, or be banished from the State, as the Court shall see fit.

SEC. 31. The Governor's duty is to require all persons who come into this State, for the purposes, and under the circumstances stated in the 1st section of the Act of '44: and the preceding 29th section of this digest, to depart from the State in 48 hours after such notice, and such persons shall thereupon be bound to depart, and failing to do so, they are guilty of a high misdemeanor, and upon conviction. are to be sentenced to be banished from the State, and to such fine and imprisonment, as the Court may think expedient. ⟨3d section.⟩

SEC. 32. Any person convicted a second or any subsequent time, under the 1st and 3d sections of the Act of '44, set out in the preceding 29th and 31st sections of this digest, is to be imprisoned not less than 7 years, to pay a fine not less than $1000, and to be banished from the State. ⟨4th section.⟩

SEC. 33. It is the duty of the Sheriff of the District to execute the sentence of banishment, by sending the offender out of the State; and if he shall return, (unless by unavoidable accident,) the Sheriff of the District where he may be found is "to hold" him in close confinement under the original sentence, until he shall enter into a recognizance to leave the State and never to return. ⟨5th section.⟩

SEC. 34. Free negroes, mulattoes, and mestizoes, entering this State as cook, steward, or mariner, or in any other employment, on board any vessel, in violation of the provisions of the 2d section of the Act of '35, and which is set out and prescribed in the 59th section of Chapter 1, of this digest, and who may be apprehended and confined by the Sheriff, are not entitled to the writ of Habeas Corpus. ⟨1st sec. Act of '44, 11 Stat. 293.⟩

SEC. 35. If the Sheriff shall by the usual posse comitatus and the civil authorities, not be able to enforce the provisions of the Act of '35, the Governor, on a requisition made on him, and signed by the Sheriff, is required to order out a sufficient number of the militia, to meet the exigency of the case, to be placed under the command of discreet officers, who shall be ordered to give the Sheriff the aid necessary to execute the said Act: ⟨2d sec. Act of '44. 11 Stat. 293.⟩

# ERRATA.

In the unavoidable hurry of revising the proof-sheets, a few errors escaped correction. Slight verbal inaccuracies, and those merely involving an inversion or omission of a letter, the intelligence of the reader will easily correct.

Page 10, line 3, for "*rita*," read "*rite*."
" " " 10, for "*suvitii*," read "*servitii*."

# INDEX.

# 52 INDEX.

Page.

FIRE ARMS. Not to be carried by persons of color,   16
Slaves not allowed to carry or use,   25
Seizure of, from slaves,   25
Mode of proceeding.   25
FORFEITURE. Of slaves,   27
FREEDOM. Question of, how tried,   8
On whom the burden of proof lies,   8
Entry of, must be made in Court,   9
Evidences of.   9, 10
FREE PERSONS OF COLOR. Entitled to all the rights
of property.   12
Their disabilities,   13
Their rights and privileges,   13
What the *term* signifies,   14, 15
Not to enter the State,   16
Penalty and proceedings,   16
Not allowed to carry weapons,   16
GAMING. With slaves, &c., unlawful,   45, 46
GAOLER. His duties, respecting runaways,   37
GUARDIAN. When and how appointed,   8
Who must have one, and who can be one   13
His relation towards his ward,   13
HARBORING. Of slaves by slaves, unlawful,   30, 31
Of runaway slaves,   45
Penalty for,   31, 45
HIRING. Slaves not to hire houses. &c.   25
Unlawful to hire to slaves.   25
Penalty and mode of proceeding.   25
Master not to hire to slaves their own time,   26
Penalty and proceedings,   26
Of slaves, by the year.   43
The duties, liabilities, &c., of the parties,   43
HUNTING. When unlawful in slaves,   31, 32
Trial and mode of proceeding,   32
IMPORTATION. Of slaves unlawful,   26, 27
Penalty and mode of proceeding.   26, 27
INDIANS. When declared to be slaves.   5
Color no evidence of being slaves,   5
Presumed to be free,   5
Deemed *white* within the meaning of the Constitution,   8
INSOLENCE. Of free person of color, how punished,   13
Of slaves, how punished.   32
INSURRECTION. Attempt to raise, how punished,   30
JUDGMENT. On issue of freedom,   9
Of the Court to be in writing.   34
To be signed by the Magistrate and freeholders.   34
To be returned to the Clerk's Office,   34
JURY. When they ought to find the party to be white,   6
When they should find him to be a mulatto,   6
When dispensed with,   6
The party may claim a Jury.   6
Persons of color cannot be Jurors,   13
LEVY. Slaves exempt from,   18
LICENSE. To retail, when granted,   47
Oath of applicants for,   47

# THE COMMITTEE ON THE JUDICIARY,

To whom were referred the Negro Law of South Carolina, collected and digested by the Hon. John Belton O'Neall, for the State Agricultural Society of South Carolina, respectfully

## REPORT:

That the compilation of law as exhibited in this work, will add to the high reputation already possessed by the compiler for learning and ability. So closely is the institution of which it treats, interwoven, not only with the social, but legal policy of the State, that the Statute Books are laden with enactments upon the subject, and the Term Books crowded with decisions interpreting such Statutes. To gather from this mass what is law, requires not merely much study, but accurate legal discrimination, rendering it neatly impossible for any but professional men to arrive at right conclusions. This work has gathered into a condensed form the Statutory Law now in existence, and has collated the most important decisions, shewing the principles upon which such statutory enactments should be interpreted. Had it been merely a compilation of law, the course of the Committee would be plain and easy, since they deem it, as such, a work worthy of much attention. But the author has added to this, the expression of his opinion, and although defering much to his long experience and acknowledged capacity, the Committee are constrained to differ widely from these views, and to express the belief that his views are such as would, if disseminated, prejudice the settled policy of the State. The Committee have been unable, from the short space of time allowed for the consideration of this work, to express as fully as was desired their views upon this subject, but they now proceed, as succinctly as possible, to state the objections which presented themselves upon a rapid review.

And the first objection which the Committee urge, is to the positive terms used in chap. 1, sec. 8, "When the blood is reduced to, or below one-eighth, the jury ought always to find the party white." The case of the State vs. Davis & Hanna, 2 Bail, 560, the strongest upon the subject, by no means support so positive an assertion. The decision goes no farther than to say, that as a general rule, it should assist the jury in finding a verdict, being in general conformable to experience, while it distinctly says, other and concurring circumstances should also be required to aid the finding of the jury. No positive law can be laid down; features, color, and other personal appearance, will often enable a jury to come to a decision, where a fixed quantity of blood would prove of little or no avail. The Committee fully concur with the opinion of the above cited case, and believe it the only true criterion upon the subject.

The expression of opinion contained in chap. 1, Sec. 15, is not to be regarded as law, but merely as the dictum of one whom the Committee frankly avow, learned and able, and whose opinion is entitled to much weight. As a general rule, the onus of proof rests upon such as claim a higher status of color, whether the same burden rests in cases of prohibition against a Tax Collector's execution, is unadjudicated. This section should not therefore be regarded as established law.

The next point upon which the Committee differ from the author, is with the reasoning contained in chap. 1, Sec. 19. The law is laid down in this section, is doubtless correct; but the argument ased to overthrow the law, are such as cannot meet the views of the Committee. Although, by the Constitution placed upon a higher status in society than the African race, many substantial reasons exist why the Indian should not be allowed to enjoy the full privileges of a white. The servile condition of the negro race, and the well established policy of the State, to exclude them from all political franchises, is of itself a strong reason why the Indian should be debarred, in this respect, from an equality with the white man. So closely does the color of those two races assimilate, that granting these privileges to one, may effect an entrance for the other, and lead to a disregard for color, the observance of which is one of the strong supports of the institution. The Indian also enjoys certain immunities, such as freedom from taxation, &c. and with his tribe constitutes, in a measure, a separate government. The allowance therefore, of suffrage and holding office would place him upon a better condition than the whites. Other reasons could be adduced, but these are deemed sufficient to show the wisdom of its decision.

The committee must also differ fiom the opinion expressed in chap. 1, sec. 44. The Acts of 1820 and 1841, prohibiting emancipation, were the result of iong experience, and forced upon the State by an abuse of the right. The creation of a class differing by no distinctive color, and but little greater immunities, from the servile class, and elated by a nominal freedom, cannot fail to produce in the lower caste envy and heart-burning, the result of which may be most disastrous. Neither can this intermediate grade be considered as a safeguard, debarred by the policy of the country from the privileges of the white man, they cannot assimilate with him in feeling, and must, to a certain extent, seek sympathy with those in a lower rank of life. The indolent character of the race, and their indisposition to labor, when livelihood can be obtained by other means, would have a tendency to create a class seriously prejudicial to the interests and morality of the community.

In chap. 1, sec. 47, it is said of Free Negroes, "their marriages with one another, and even with white people, are legal." The case of Bowers vs. Newman, 2 McMullan, p. 472, cited in the margin, as an authority for this expression, by no means supports the position. It was not deemed necessary by Judge Earle, who delivered the opinion of the Court in this case, to consider the legality of such marriages, and in this he was sustained by five Judges ; two dissentient opinions were delivered, in which the point was considered, and said to be legal. But, as the case turned upon other points, the opinion of two of the Court cannot be considered as decisive, and more especially so, since a majority of the Bench did not deem it a question in issue, although learnedly argued before them. The legality of such marriages has therefore been unadjudicated, and the Committee will now proceed to give reasons why they deem such marriages between whites and colored persons illegal. The arguments upon this subject in the Carolina Law Journal, p. 92, and seq , so forcible that no apology is deemed necessary for extracting therefrom. Marriages between slaves is treated as concubinage, merely from the incapacity of the slave to contract. Marriages between whites and colored persons is next considered, and classed also as concubinage. "The universal difference," says the author, "between concubinage and marriage, is the want of inter-communication of civil rights and privileges—equality of *status.*" "Their contract, therefore, is not marriage; it can, at best, amount only to what was concubinage by mutual contract under the civil law." "A colored man, though no slave, is not *sui juris*; he must have a guardian appointed; he must act through his guardian." "Under such marriage contract, the guardian of the colored women and the husband may be two different persons." Strong as these arguments undoubtedly are, they appear strengthened by the effect of the decision in the State vs. Hayes, 1 Bail., p. 275, that the offspring of a white female by a colored male is a mulatto, and can be tried only in a Court of Magistrate and Freeholders. Can that connection be legal then, which deprives the issue of a white, whose color gives certain privileges? Or must it not be concubinage merely? But again, one of the incidents of marriage, under the common law, is to put a woman under control of her husband, *"fustibus et flagellis aerita verberare uxorom."* Can the connection be legal, which, in case of correction on the husband's part, would at once subject him to indictment for striking a white? But apart from the reasons which would induce the belief that the marriages between whites and colored persons are illegal, the policy of the State is decidedly against it. Whatever tends to break down the barriers between the two classes of color, must weaken the institution.

Whether free negroes are entitled to the writ of *Habeas Corpus*, is yet undecided. At *Nisi Prius* the writ has been allowed, but no case, in the knowledge of the Committee, has been presented to the Court of Appeals requiring a decision. The Committee, therefore thing the law is too positively laid down in chap. 1. sec. 48.

With the reasoning contained in chap. 1, Sec. 52, the Committee feel called upon to differ. The obligation of an oath is too great to be administered to a class so illiterate as to be unable to understand its nature, and whose proverbial mendacity would generally lead to its violation.

The term "freeman" used in the Constitution, does not, in the opinion of the Committee, apply to free persons of color. The imposition of a capitation tax, has been always deemed a healthy regulation, and in case of failure to pay it, the law has affixed a penalty but little different from that attached to a white man, who begets a bastard, and is unable to pay the sentence. The Committee consequently cannot agree with the author, in chap. 1, sec. 55, that the Constitutionality of the law is doubtful.

The policy of the State in excluding from its limits by stringent laws, free negroes and persons of color, coming from other places, is so firmly established, and their wisdom so generally conceded, that no reasoning is needed on the part of the Committee for differing in opinion from the author in chap. 1. sec. 65.

Neither can the Committee agree in the opinion expressed in chap. 2, sec. 8, relative to a mitigation of the law against such as inveigle and steal negroes. Recent events have demonstrated that fanaticism will go to such extreme lengths, as to need laws of a most penal character, for self defence.

The provision of the County Court Act, exempting Slaves from levy under certain circumstances, has not, in the belief of the Committee, been repealed; they cannot therefore coincide in the doubt expressed in chap. 2 sec. 9, whether it remains of force.

The Committee express a decided dissent, to the charge brought in chap. 2. sec. 26, that the negroes in South Carolina are so badly provided with clothing, food, &c., as to need the enforcement of the existing statutory enactments by severe penalties. As a peasantry, their provision is probably more ample, than in any other part of the world, except the slaveholding States; a provision so ample, that even the existing laws are a dead letter upon the Statute books. Independently of the feeling of humanity, it is the interest of all who hold this property, to make such arrangements for comfort, as will both preserve health, strength and life, and contribute to their increase. The exceptions, if any exist, must be very rare. Constituted of persons from all sections of the State, whose professional avocations lead them to mingle freely with their respective constituencies, the Committee are not aware of any part of the State, where the instincts of humanity are dead, or the dictates of interest unheeded.

The causes which led to the Act of 1834, making it an indictable offence to teach slaves to read or write, have by no means abated, but rather increased. The committee therefore cannot concur with the opinion expressed in chap. 2. sec. 42; nor is the slave by such prohibition cut off from learning the doctrines of Christianity. Apart from any instructions which may be communicated by the owner or his family, domestic missionaries have within the last few years been rapidly extending their work; and there are now opportunities afforded in almost every part of the State, for negroes to attend Divine worship, and be instructed. And a large number of planters, steadily employ ministers, to perform service on the Sabbath, and teach their slaves the elements of Christianity.

The Acts mentioned in chap. 2, sec. 47, the Committee cannot believe should be repealed. While it is true that religious meetings are allowed, and the enactments virtually repealed, still they should remain, that in case of necessity the law may be enforced, and protection afforded to both whites and blacks. The same reason applies to sec. 52.

Chap. 3, sec. 23, would, in the opinion of the Committee, have been more complete, had it been stated that under the Act of 1839, four of the Freeholders and the Magistrate could sign Judgment.

By the Act of 1847, the Patrol system was abolished, within certain limits on Charleston neck, and a police authorized: the 55th sec. of chap. 3, would have been more perfect by a notice of this Statute.

In discharging the duty assigned to them, the Committee are sensible that some points have been passed over, on which the author held opinions different from the Committee. The brief time allowed for the work, rendered an answer to all, impracticable: and the Committee deemed it most beneficial to notice such as seemed most objectionable. The Committee reiterate their belief that as a compilation of law it is valuable, and generally correct. But the incorporation of private opinions, however high the source from which they emanate, may tend to lead the unskilled into error.

The Committee therefore recommend that it is inexpedient that the work should be printed, at the expense of the State, since in many particulars, it contains opinions at variance with the settled policy of the State.

WILMOT G. DESAUSSURE, On behalf of the Committee.